"The Story of Jesus"

Originally published under the title *Life of Christ*
Abridged Edition Revised Copyright 1976, Paul C. Brownlow
ISBN: 0-915720-18-3

Presented to:

_____

_____

By:

_____

_____

_____ 19____

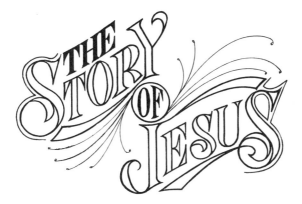

JAMES STALKER

Illustrations by Gary Day McCaleb

BROWNLOW PUBLISHING COMPANY, INC.
P. O. Box 3141
Fort Worth, Texas 76105

Brownlow Gift Books

Contents

Foreword

It is the aim of this volume — *The Story of Jesus* — to bring into prominence the great masses of our Lord's life, and clearly point out its hinge-events, curtailing details as much as possible. What most readers of the Gospels need is a design let down on the details, so that the life of Jesus may present itself to the eye as a whole; and an endeavor is made in *The Story of Jesus* to supply this want. For the reader who desires more details we have given Scripture citations at the conclusion of various paragraphs.

No other book, so far as the publishers are aware, has been written on the plan of this one—to exhibit in the briefest possible space the main features and the general course of the life of Jesus, so as to cause the times, the circumstances and the well-known facts of His life to flow together in the reader's mind and shape themselves into an easily comprehensible whole. This view is essential if one would see the real picture, which is apt to be missed in the voluminous volumes absorbed with the details of the life of the Man of Nazareth.

This book was first published in 1880, in England, under the title, *The Life of Jesus Christ*. Some studies may disagree with the author's major chronological divisions. However, the facts in the life of Christ are more important than their chronology; so scholarship's not being fully agreed on the exact order of every event in our Lord's life is no major issue. In this present edition we have deleted approximately a third of the original words for the sake of brevity and directness; have divided the former six chapters into thirteen; and have added the Scripture references which were not given by the author. Also, in the paperback, class edition, we have given a review exercise at the conclusion of each chapter to facilitate class studies.

Convinced that no person is truly educated who is unknowledgeable of the world's most influential character; and believing that this marvelous book has a most vital mission to give a broader understanding of this famous One, we present it to the public with the highest anticipations.

THE PUBLISHERS

One Man's Life

Here is a young man who was born in an obscure village, the child of a peasant woman. He grew up in another village. He worked in a carpenter shop until he was thirty, and then for three years he was an itinerant preacher. He never wrote a book. He never held an office. He never owned a home. He never had a family. . .

He never went to college. He never put his foot inside a big city. He never traveled 200 miles from the place where he was born. He never did one of the things that usually accompany greatness. He had no credentials but himself. . .

While he was still a young man the tide of public opinion turned against him. His friends ran away. He was turned over to his enemies. He went through the mockery of a trial.

He was nailed to the cross between two thieves. While he was dying, his executioners gambled for the only piece of property he had on earth, and that was his coat.

When he was dead he was laid in a borrowed grave through the pity of a friend. Nineteen centuries wide have come and gone, and today he is the central figure of the human race and the leader of the column of progress. . .

All the armies that ever marched and all the navies that ever sailed, and all the parliaments that ever sat, and all the kings that ever reigned, put together, have not affected the life of man upon this earth as has that one solitary life.

ONE

The Nativity

THE BIRTH

Augustus was sitting on the throne of the Roman empire, and the touch of his finger could set the machinery of government in motion over well-nigh the whole of the civilized world. He was proud of his power and wealth, and it was one of his favorite occupations to compile a register of the populations and revenues of his vast dominions. So he issued an edict, as Luke says, "that all the world should be taxed," or to express accurately what the words probably mean, that a census, to serve as a basis for future taxation, should be taken of all his subjects. (Luke 2:1)

One of the countries affected by this decree was Palestine, whose king, Herod the Great, was a vassal of Augustus. It set the whole land in motion; for, in accordance with ancient Jewish custom, the census was taken, not at the places where the inhabitants were at the time residing, but at the places to which they belonged as members of the original twelve tribes. (Luke 2:3)

Among those whom the edict of Augustus drove forth to the highways were a humble pair in the Galilean village of Nazareth—Joseph, the carpenter of the village, and Mary, his espoused wife. They had to go a journey of nearly a hundred miles in order to inscribe themselves in the proper register; for, though peasants, they had the blood of kings in their veins, and belonged to the ancient and royal town of Bethlehem, in the far south of the country. (Luke 2:4,5)

Day by day the emperor's will, like an invisible hand, forced them southward along the weary road, till at last they climbed the rocky ascent that led to the gate of the town,—he terrified with anxiety, and she well-nigh dead with fatigue. They reached the inn, but found it crowded with strangers, who, bent on the same errand as themselves, had arrived before them. No friendly house opened its door to receive them, and they were fain to clear for their lodging a corner of the inn-yard, else occupied by the beasts of the numerous travelers. There, that very night, she brought forth her first-born Son; and because there was neither womanly hand to assist her, nor couch to receive Him, she wrapped Him in swaddling-clothes and laid Him in a manger. (Luke 2:7)

Next morning the noise and bustle broke out again in the inn and inn-yard; the citizens of Bethlehem went about their work; the registration proceeded; and in the meantime the greatest event in the history of the world had taken place. We never know where a great beginning may be happening. Every arrival of a new soul in the world is a mystery and a shut casket of possibilities. Joseph and Mary alone knew the tremendous secret— that on her, the peasant maiden and carpenter's bride, had been conferred the honor of being the mother of Him who was the Messiah of her race, the Savior of the world, and the Son of God. (Matthew 1:21)

It had been foretold in ancient prophecy that He should be born on this very spot: "But thou, Bethlehem Ephratah, though thou be little among the thousands of Judah, yet out of thee shall He come forth unto me that is to be ruler in Israel." The proud emperor's decree affected the anxious couple. Yes; but another hand was leading them on—the hand of Him who overrules the purposes of emperors and kings, of statesmen and parliaments, for the accomplishment of His designs, though they know them not; who could overrule for His own far-reaching purpose the pride and ambition of Augustus. (Micah 5:2; Matthew 2:13-15)

THE GROUP AROUND THE INFANT

Although Jesus made His entry on the stage of life so humbly and silently; although the citizens of Bethlehem dreamed not what had happened in their midst; although the emperor of Rome knew not that his decree had influenced the nativity of a king who was yet to bear rule, not only over the Roman world, but over many a land where Rome's eagles never flew; although the history of mankind went thundering forward next morning in the channels of its ordinary interests, quite unconscious of the event which had happened, yet it did not altogether escape notice.

That which was unnoticed by the kings and great ones of this world was so absorbing a theme to the angels that they burst the bonds of the invisibility in which they shroud themselves, in order to express their joy and ex-

plain the significance of the great event. And seeking
the most worthy hearts to which they might communi-
cate it, they found them in simple shepherds, living the
life of contemplation and prayer in the suggestive fields
where Jacob had kept his flocks, where Boaz and Ruth
had been wedded, and where David, the great Old Testament type, had spent his youth, and there, by the study
of the secrets and needs of their own hearts, learning far
more of the nature of the Savior who was to come than
the Pharisee amidst the religious pomp of the temple, or
the scribe burrowing without the seeing eye among the
prophecies of the Old Testament. The angel directed them
where the Savior was, and they hastened to the town to
find Him. They were the representatives of the peasant
people, with the "honest and good heart," who afterwards formed the bulk of His disciples. (Luke 2:8-18)

On the eighth day after His birth, the Child was cir-
cumcised, thus being "made under the law," entering into
the covenant, and inscribing His name in His own blood
in the roll of the nation. Soon thereafter, when the days
of Mary's purification were ended, they carried Him
from Bethlehem to Jerusalem to present Him to the Lord
in the temple. It was "the Lord of the temple entering
the temple of the Lord"; but few visitors to the spot
could have been less noticed by the priests, for Mary, instead of offering the sacrifice usual in such cases, could
only afford two turtle doves, the offering of the poor.
Yet there were eyes looking on, undazzled by the shows
and glitter of the world, from which His poverty could
not conceal Him. (Luke 2:21,22; Leviticus 12:1-8)

Simeon an aged saint who in answer to many prayers
had received a secret promise that he should not die till

he had seen the Messiah, met the parents and the child, when suddenly it shot through him like a flash of lightning that this at last was He, and, taking Him up in his arms, he praised God for the advent of the Light to lighten the Gentiles and the Glory of His people Israel. While he was still speaking, another witness joined the group. It was Anna a saintly widow who literally dwelt in the courts of the Lord, and had purified the eye of her spirit with the euphrasy and rue of prayer and fasting till it could pierce with prophetic glance the veils of sense. She united her testimony to the old man's, praising God and confirming the mighty secret to the other expectant souls who were looking for redemption in Israel. (Luke 2:25-38)

The shepherds and these aged saints were near the spot where the new force entered the world. But it thrilled susceptible souls at a much greater distance. It was probably after the presentation in the temple and after the parents had carried back their child to Bethlehem, where it was their intention to reside instead of returning to Nazareth, that He was visited by the Wise Men of the East. These were members of the learned class of the Magians, the repositories of science, philosophy, medical skill, and religious mysteries in the countries beyond the Euphrates. Tacitus, Suetonius, and Josephus tell us that in the regions from whence they came, there then prevailed an expectation that a great king was to arise in Judea. We know also from the calculations of the great astronomer Kepler, that at this very time there was visible in the heavens a brilliant temporary star.

Now the Magi were ardent students of astrology, and believed that any unusual phenomenon in the heavens was the sign of some remarkable event on earth; and it is possible that, connecting this star, to which their attention would undoubtedly be eagerly directed, with the expectation mentioned by the ancient historians, they were led westward to see if it had been fulfilled. But there must also have been awakened in them a deeper want, to which God responded. If their search began in scientific curiosity and speculation, God led it on to the perfect truth. (Matthew 2:1,2)

All these gathered round the Holy Child,—the shepherds with their simple wonder, Simeon and Anna with a reverence enriched by the treasured wisdom and piety of centuries, and the wise men with the lavish gifts of the Orient and the open brow of Gentile knowledge. But while these worthy worshippers were gazing down on Him, there was a sinister and murderous man conniving and plotting. It was Herod. This prince then occupied the throne of the country. His subjects hated him, and it was only by Roman favor that he was maintained in his seat. He was able, ambitious, and magnificent. Yet he had such a cruel, crafty, gloomy, and filthy mind. He had been guilty of every crime. He had made his very palace swim in blood, having murdered his own favorite wife, three of his sons, and many others of his relatives. He was now old and tortured with disease, remorse, the sense of unpopularity, and a cruel terror of every possible aspirant to the throne which he had usurped.

The wise men had naturally turned their steps to the capital, to inquire where He was to be born whose sign they had seen in the East. The suggestion touched Herod in his sorest place; but with diabolical hypocrisy he concealed his suspicions. Having learned from the priests that the Messiah was to be born in Bethlehem, he directed the Magi thither, but arranged that they should return and tell him the very house where the new King was. He hoped to cut Him off at a single blow. But he was foiled; for, being warned by God, they did not come back to tell him, but returned to their own country another way. Then his fury burst forth like a storm, and he sent his soldiers to murder every babe under two years of age in Bethlehem. As well might he have attempted to cut a mountain of adamant asunder as cut the chain of the divine purposes. "He thrust his sword into the nest, but the bird was flown." Joseph fled with the Child to Egypt, and remained there till Herod died, when he returned and dwelt at Nazareth; being warned from Bethlehem, because there he would have been in the kingdom of Archelaus, the like-minded son of his bloodthirsty father. Herod's murderous intent was a sad beginning of how the powers of the world would persecute Him and cut off His life from the earth. (Matthew 2:1-15)

Joseph and Mary fled with the Child to Egypt.

TWO

The Silent Years

LACK OF RECORDS

The records which we possess up to this point are, as we have seen, comparatively full. But with the settlement at Nazareth, after the return from Egypt, our information comes to a sudden stop, and over the rest of the life of Jesus, till His public ministry begins, a thick covering is drawn, which is only lifted once. We should have wished the narrative to continue with the same fulness through the years of His boyhood and youth. What would we not give to know the habits, the friendships, the thoughts, the words, and the actions of Jesus during so many years? But it has pleased God, whose silence is no less wonderful than His words, to keep it shut except for one incident. (Luke 2:40-52)

It was natural that, where God was silent and curiosity was strong, the fancy of man should attempt to fill up the blank. Accordingly, in the early church there appeared Apocryphal Gospels, pretending to give full details where the inspired Gospels were silent. They are particularly full of the sayings and doings of the childhood of Jesus. But they only show how unequal the human imagination was to such a theme, and bring out by the contrast of glitter and caricature the solidity and truthfulness of the Scripture narrative. They make him a worker of frivolous and useless marvels, who moulded birds of clay and made them fly, changed his playmates into kids, and so forth. In short, they are compilations of worthless and often blasphemous fables.

These grotesque failures warn us not to intrude with the suggestions of fancy into the hallowed enclosure. It is enough to know that He grew in wisdom and stature, and in favor with God and man. He was a real child and youth, and passed through all the stages of a natural development. Body and mind grew together, the one expanding to manly vigor, and the other acquiring more and more knowledge and power. His opening character exhibited a grace that made every one who saw it wonder and love its goodness and purity. (Deuteronomy 29:29)

HIS HOME

We know amidst what kind of home influences He was brought up. His home was one of those which were the glory of His country, as they are of our own—the abodes of the godly and intelligent working class. Joseph, its head, was a man saintly and wise; but the fact that he is not mentioned in Christ's afterlife has generally been believed to indicate that he died during the youth of Jesus, perhaps leaving the care of the household on His shoulders. His mother probably exercised the most decisive of all external influences on His development. What she was may be inferred from the fact that she was chosen from all the women of the world to be crowned with the supreme honor of womanhood. The song which she poured forth on the subject of her own great destiny shows her to have been a woman religious, fervently poetical, and patriotic; a student of scripture, and especially of its great women, for it is saturated with Old Testament ideas, and moulded on Hannah's song; a spirit exquisitely humble, yet capable of thoroughly appreciating the honor conferred upon her. She was no miraculous queen of heaven, as superstition has caricatured her, but a woman exquisitely pure, saintly, loving, and high-souled. This is aureole enough. Jesus grew up in her love and passionately returned it. (Luke 1:38-56; Matthew 1:18-25)

There were other inmates of the household. He had brothers and sisters. It is not likely that they were close companions to Him in Nazareth. He was probably much alone; and the pathos of His saying, that a prophet is not without honor save in his own country and in his own house, probably reached back into the years before His ministry began. (Matthew 13:55-57)

EDUCATIONAL INFLUENCES

He received His education at home, or from a scribe attached to the village synagogue. It was only, however, a poor man's education. As the scribes contemptuously said, He had never learned, or, as we should say, He was not college-bred. No; but the love of knowledge was early awake within Him. He daily knew the joy of deep and happy thought; He had the best of all keys to knowledge —the open mind and the loving heart; and the three great books lay ever open before Him—the Bible, Man, and Nature. (John 7:15)

It is easy to understand with what fervent enthusiasm He would devote Himself to the Old Testament; and His sayings, which are full of quotations from it, afford abundant proof of how constantly it formed the food of His mind and the comfort of His soul. His youthful study of it was the secret of the marvelous facility with which He made use of it afterwards in order to enrich His preaching and enforce His doctrine, to repel the assaults of opponents and overcome the temptations of the Evil One. (Matthew 4:1-10)

There are few places where human nature can be better studied than in a country village; for there one sees the whole of each individual life and knows all one's neighbors thoroughly. In a city far more people are seen, but far fewer known; it is only the outside of life that is visible. In a village the view outwards is circumscribed; but the view downwards is deep, and the view upwards unimpeded. Nazareth was a notoriously wicked town, as we learn from the proverbial question, "Can any good thing come out of Nazareth?" Jesus had no acquaintance with sin in His own soul, but in the town He had a full exhibition of the awful problem with which it was to be His life-work to deal. (John 1:46)

He was still further brought into contact with human nature by His trade. That He worked as a carpenter in Joseph's shop there can be no doubt. Who could know better than His own townsmen, who asked, in their astonishment at His preaching, "Is not this the carpenter?" It would be difficult to exhaust the significance of the fact that God chose for His Son, when He dwelt among men, out of all the possible positions in which He might have placed Him, the lot of a working man. It stamped men's common toils with everlasting honor. It acquainted Jesus with the feelings of the multitude, and helped Him to know what was in man. It was afterwards said that He knew this so well that He needed not that any man should teach Him. (Mark 6:3; John 2:25)

Travelers tell us that the spot where He grew up is one of the most beautiful on the face of the earth. Nazareth is situated in a secluded, cup-like valley amid the mountains of Zebulon, just where they dip down into the plain of Esdraelon, with which it is connected by a steep and rocky path. Its white houses, with vines clinging to their walls, are embowered amidst gardens and groves of olive, fig, orange, and pomegranate trees. The fields are divided by hedges of cactus, and enamelled with innumerable flowers of every hue. Behind the village rises a hill five hundred feet in height, from whose summit there is seen one of the most wonderful views in the world—the mountains of Galilee, with snowy Hermon towering above them, to the north; the ridge of Carmel, the coast of Tyre, and the sparkling waters of the Mediterranean, to the west; a few miles to the east, the wooded, cone-like bulk of Tabor; and to the south, the plain of Esdraelon, with the mountains of Ephraim beyond. (Luke 2:51; 4:16)

The preaching of Jesus shows how deeply He had drunk into the essence of natural beauty and revelled in the changing aspects of the seasons. It was when wandering as a lad in these fields that He gathered the images of beauty which he poured out in His parables and addresses. It was on that hill that He acquired the habit of retreating to the mountain-tops to spend the night in solitary prayer. The doctrines of His preaching were poured out in a living stream when the occasion came, but the water had been gathered into the hidden well for many years before. In the fields and on the mountainside he had gleaned much during the years of happy and undisturbed meditation and prayer.

There is still one important educational influence to be mentioned. Every year, after He was twelve years old, He went with His parents to the Passover at Jerusalem. Fortunately we have preserved to us an account of the first of these visits. It is the only occasion on which the veil is lifted during thirty years. (Luke 2:41-50; Exodus 12:1-30)

Every one who can remember his own first journey from a village home to the capital of his country will understand the joy and excitement with which Jesus set out. He traveled over eighty miles of a country where nearly every mile teemed with historical and inspiring memories. He mingled with the constantly growing caravan of pilgrims, who were filled with the religious enthusiasm of the great ecclesiastical event of the year. His destination was a city which was loved by every Jewish heart with a strength of affection that has never been given to any other capital—a city full of objects and memories fitted to touch the deepest springs of interest and emotion in his breast. It was swarming at the Passover-time with strangers from half-a-hundred countries, speaking as many languages and wearing as many different costumes. He went to take part for the first time in an ancient solemnity suggestive of countless patriotic and sacred memories.

It was no wonder that, when the day came to return home, He was so excited with the new objects of interest, that He failed to join His party at the appointed place and time. One spot above all fascinated His interest. It was the temple, and especially the school there in which the masters of wisdom taught. His mind was teeming with questions which these doctors might be asked to answer. His thirst for knowledge had an opportunity for the first time to drink its fill. So it was there His anxious parents, who, missing Him after a day's journey northward, returned in anxiety to seek Him, found Him, listening with excited looks to the oracles of the wisdom of the day. His answer to the reproachful question of His mother lays bare His childhood's mind. It shows that already, though so young, He had risen above the great mass of men, who drift on through life without once inquiring what may be its meaning and its end. He was aware that He had a God-appointed life-work to do, which it was the one business of His existence to accomplish. It was the passionate thought for the rest of His life. It ought to be the first and last thought of every life. It recurred again and again in His later sayings, and pealed itself finally forth in the word with which He closed His career,—It is finished! (Matthew 26:39; John 19:30)

It has often been asked whether Jesus knew all along that He was the Messiah, and, if not, when and how the knowledge dawned upon Him; whether it was suggested by hearing from His mother the story of His birth, or announced to Him from within. Did it dawn upon Him all at once, or gradually? When did the plan of His career, which He carried out so unhesitatingly from the beginning of His ministry, shape itself in His mind? Was it the slow result of years of reflection, or did it come to Him at once? These questions have occupied the greatest Christian minds and received very various answers. I will not venture to answer them, and especially with His reply to His mother before me, I can not trust myself even to think of a time when He did not know what His work in this world was to be.

His subsequent visits to Jerusalem must have greatly influenced the development of His mind. If He often went back to hear and question the rabbis in the temple schools, He must soon have discovered how shallow was their far-famed learning. It was probably on these annual visits that He discovered the utter corruption of the religion of the day and the need of a radical reform of both doctrine and practice, and marked the practices and the persons that He was by and by to assail with the vehemence of His holy indignation.

Such were the external conditions amidst which the manhood of Jesus waxed towards maturity. It would be easy to exaggerate the influence which they may be supposed to have exerted on his development. The greater and more original a character is, the less dependent is it on the peculiarities of its environment. It is fed from deep well-springs within itself, and in its germ there is a type enclosed which expands in obedience to its own laws and bids defiance to circumstances. In any other circumstances, Jesus would have grown to be in every important respect the very same person as He became in Nazareth.

THREE

The Nation and the Time

We now approach the time when, after thirty years of silence and obscurity in Nazareth, Jesus was to step forth on the public stage. Every great biography is the record of the entrance into the world of a new force, bringing with it something different from all that was there before, and of the way in which it gradually gets itself incorporated with the old, so as to become a part of the future. Obviously, therefore, two things are needed by those who wish to understand it—first, a clear comprehension of the nature of the new force itself; and secondly, a view of the world with which it is to be incorporated. Jesus brought with Him into the world more that was original and destined to modify the future history of mankind than any one else who has ever entered it. But we can neither understand Him nor the fortunes which He encountered in seeking to incorporate with history the gift He brought, without a clear view of the condition of the sphere within which His life was to be passed.

POLITICAL CONDITION

Politically, the nation had passed through extra-ordinary vicissitudes. After the Exile, it had been organized as a kind of sacred State under its high priests; but conqueror after conqueror had since marched over it, changing everything; the old hereditary monarchy had been restored for a time by the brave Maccabees; the battle of freedom had many times been won and lost, and now at last the country was completely under the mighty Roman power, which had extended its sway over the whole civilized world. Roman soldiers paraded the streets of Jerusalem; Roman standards waved over the country; Roman tax-gatherers sat at the gate of every town. To the Sanhedrin, the supreme Jewish organ of government, only a shadow of power was still conceded, its presidents, the high priests, being mere puppets of Rome, set up and put down with the utmost caprice. So low had the proud nation fallen whose ideal it had ever been to rule the world, and whose patriotism was a religious and national passion as intense and unquenchable as ever burned in any country.

RELIGIOUS AND SOCIAL CONDITION

In religion the changes had been equally great, and the fall equally low. In external appearance, indeed, it might have seemed as if progress had been made instead of retrogression. The nation was far more orthodox than it had been at many earlier periods of its history. Once its chief danger had been idolatry; but the chastisement of the Exile had corrected that tendency for ever, and thenceforward the Jews, wherever they might be living, were uncompromising monotheists. The priestly orders and offices had been thoroughly reorganized after the return from Babylon, and the temple services and annual feasts continued to be observed at Jerusalem with strict regularity.

Besides, a new and most important religious institution had arisen, which almost threw the temple with its priesthood into the background. This was the synagogue with its rabbis. It does not seem to have existed in ancient times at all, but was called into existence after the Exile. Synagogues were multiplied wherever Jews lived; every Sabbath they were filled with praying congregations; exhortations were delivered by the rabbis—a new order created by the need of expounders to translate from the Hebrew, which had become a dead language; and nearly the whole Old Testament was read over once a year in the hearing of the people. Schools of theology, similar to our divinity halls, had sprung up, in which the rabbis were trained and the sacred books interpreted. (Synagogues appear to have arisen during the exile, in the abeyance of the temple-worship, and to have received their full development on the return of the Jews from captivity. The whole history of Ezra presupposes the habit of solemn, probably of periodic, meetings. Ezra 8:15; Nehemiah 8:2; 9:1; Zechariah 7:5. After the Maccabean struggle for independence, we find almost every town or village had its one or more synagogues.—*Smith's Bible Dictionary*)

But, in spite of all this religiosity, religion had sadly declined. The externals had been multiplied, but the inner spirit had disappeared. However rude and sinful the old nation had sometimes been, it was capable in its worst periods of producing majestic religious figures, who kept high the ideal of life and preserved the connection of the nation with Heaven; and the inspired voices of the prophets kept the stream of truth running fresh and clean. But during four hundred years no prophet's voice had been heard from Malichi's time to Christ's time. The records of the old prophetic utterances were still preserved with almost idolatrous reverence, but there were not men to understand what He had formerly written. (Matthew 15:8)

The representative religious men of the time were the Pharisees. As their name indicates, they originally arose as champions of the separateness of the Jews from other nations. This was a noble idea, so long as the distinction emphasized was holiness. But it is far more difficult to maintain this distinction than such external differences as peculiarities of dress, food, language, etc. These were in course of time substituted for it. The Pharisees were ardent patriots, ever hating the foreign yoke with impassioned bitterness. They despised other races, and clung with undying faith to the hope of a glorious future for their nation. But they had so long harped on this idea, that they had come to believe themselves the special favorites of Heaven, simply because they were descendants of Abraham, and to lose sight of the importance of personal character. They multiplied their Jewish peculiarities, but substituted external observances, such as fasts, prayers, tithes, washings, sacrifices, and so forth, for the grand distinctions of love to God and love to man. (Matthew 23:5; 3:7-9; 6:1-18; John 4:9)

To the Pharisaic party belonged most of the scribes. They were so called because they were both the interpreters and copyists of the Scriptures and the lawyers of the people; for, the Jewish legal code being incorporated in the Holy Scriptures, jurisprudence became a branch of theology. They were the chief interpreters in the synagogues, although any male worshipper was permitted to speak if he chose. They professed unbounded reverence for the Scriptures, counting every word and letter in them. They had a splendid opportunity of diffusing the religious principles of the Old Testament among the people; for the synagogue was one of the most potent engines of instruction ever devised by any people. But they entirely missed their opportunity. They became a dry ecclesiastical and scholastic class, using their position for selfish aggrandisement, and scorning those to whom they gave stones for bread as a vulgar and unlettered *canaille*. Whatever was most spiritual, living, human, and grand in the Scriptures they passed by. Generation after generation the commentaries of their famous men multiplied, and the pupils studied the commentaries instead of the text. Moreover, it was a rule with them that the correct interpretation of a passage was as authoritative as the text itself; and, the interpretations of the famous masters being as a matter of course believed to be correct, the mass of opinions which were held to be as precious as the Bible itself grew to enormous proportions. These were "the traditions of the elders." (Matthew 15:1-14; 23:14-27; Mark 7:1-13)

By degrees an arbitrary system of exegesis came into vogue, by which almost any opinion whatever could be thus connected with some text and stamped with divine authority. Every new invention of Pharisaic peculiarities was sanctioned in this way. This was the chaff with which they fed the people in the synagogues. The conscience was burdened with innumerable details, every one of which was represented to be as divinely sanctioned as any of the ten commandments. This was the intolerable burden which Peter said neither he nor his fathers had been able to bear. This was the horrible nightmare which sat so long on Paul's conscience. But worse consequences flowed from it. It is a well-known principle in history, that, whenever the ceremonial is elevated to the same rank with the moral, the latter will soon be lost sight of. The scribes and Pharisees had learned how by arbitrary exegesis and casuistical discussion to explain away the weightiest moral obligations, and make up for the neglect of them by increasing their ritual observances. Society was rotten with vice within, and veneered over with a self-deceptive religiosity without. (Luke 18:10-14; Acts 15:10)

There was a party of protest. The Sadducees impugned the authority attached to the traditions of the fathers, demanding a return to the Bible and nothing but the Bible, and cried out for morality in place of ritual. But their protest was prompted merely by the spirit of denial, and not by a warm opposite principle of religion. They were sceptical, cold-hearted, worldly men. Though they praised morality, it was a morality unwarmed and unilluminated by any contact with that upper region of divine forces from which the inspiration of the highest morality must always come. They refused to burden their consciences with the painful punctilios of the Pharisees; but it was because they wished to live the life of comfort and self-indulgence. They mingled freely with the Gentiles, affected Greek culture, enjoyed foreign amusements, and thought it useless to fight for the freedom of their country. An extreme section of them were the Herodians, who had given in to the usurpation of Herod, and with courtly flattery attached themselves to the favor of his sons. (Matthew 16:1,6,11,12; 22:16,23)

The Sadduccees belonged chiefly to the upper and wealthy classes. The Pharisees and scribes formed what we should call the middle class, although also deriving many members from the higher ranks of life. The lower classes and the country people were separated by a great gulf from their wealthy neighbors, but attached themselves by admiration to the Pharisees, as the uneducated always do to the party of warmth. Down below all these was a large class of those who had lost all connection with religion and well-ordered social life—the publicans, harlots, and sinners, for whose souls no man cared. (Matthew 21:31,32)

Such were the pitiable features of the society on which Jesus was about to discharge His influence—a nation enslaved; the upper classes devoting themselves to selfishness, courtiership, and scepticism; the teachers and chief professors of religion lost in mere shows of ceremonialism, and boasting themselves the favorites of God, while their souls were honeycombed with self-deception and vice; the body of the people misled by false ideals; and seething at the bottom of society, a neglected mass of unblushing and unrestrained sin.

MESSIANIC HOPES

And this was the people of God! Yes; in spite of their awful degradation, these were the children of Abraham,

Isaac and Jacob, and the heirs of the covenant and the promises. Away back beyond the centuries of degradation towered the figures of the patriarchs, the kings after God's own heart, the psalmists, the prophets, the generations of faith and hope. Ay, and in front there was greatness too! The word of God could not return to Him void. He had said that to this nation was to be given the perfect revelation of Himself, that in it was to appear the perfect ideal of manhood, and that from it was to issue forth the regeneration of all mankind. Therefore a wonderful future still belonged to it. The time of fulfilment was at hand, much as the signs of the times might seem to forbid the hope. Had not all the prophets from Moses onward spoken of a great One to come, who, appearing just when the darkness was blackest and the degradation deepest, was to bring back the lost glory of the past? (Deuteronomy 18:15; Galatians 3:16-19)

So not a few faithful souls asked themselves in the weary and degraded time. There are good men in the worst of periods. There were good men even in the selfish and corrupt Jewish parties. But especially does piety linger in such epochs in the lowly homes of the people; so among the common people of Palestine there were those who, hearing the Scriptures read in the synagogues and reading them in their homes, instinctively neglected the cumbrous and endless comments of their teachers, and saw the glory of the past, of holiness and of God, which the scribes failed to see.

It was especially to the promises of a Deliverer that such spirits attached their interest. Feeling bitterly the shame of national slavery, the hollowness of the times, and the awful wickedness which rotted under the surface of society, they longed and prayed for the advent of the coming One and the restoration of the national character and glory. (John 1:41; 4:25)

The scribes also busied themselves with this element in the Scriptures. But they had caricatured the prophetic utterances on the subject by their arbitrary interpretations, and painted the future in colors borrowed from their own carnal imaginations. They spoke of the advent as the coming of the kingdom of God, and of the Messiah as the Son of God. But what they chiefly expected Him to do was, by the working of marvels and by irresistible force, to free the nation from servitude and raise it to the utmost worldly grandeur. They entertained no doubt that, simply because they were members of the chosen nation, they would be allotted high places in the kingdom, and never suspected that any change was needed in themselves to meet Him. The spiritual elements of the better time, holiness and love, were lost in their minds behind the dazzling forms of material glory.

Such was the aspect of Jewish history at the time when the hour of realizing the national destiny was about to strike. It imparted to the work which lay before the Messiah a peculiar complexity. Instead of meeting a nation mature in holiness and consecrated to the heaven-ordained task of blessing all other peoples, which He might easily lead up to its own final development, and then lead forth to the spiritual conquest of the world, He found that the first work which lay before Him was to proclaim a reformation in His own country, and encounter the opposition of prejudices that had accumulated there through centuries of degradation.

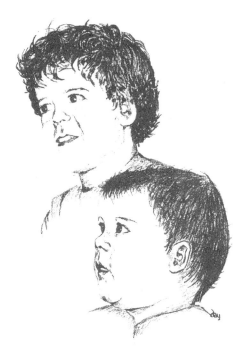

"Let the little children come to me."

FOUR

The Final Preparation

PREPARED FOR YEARS

Meanwhile He, whom so many in their own ways were hoping for, was in the midst of them, though they suspected it not. Little could they think that He about whom they were speculating and praying was growing up in a carpenter's home away in despised Nazareth. Yet so it was. There He was preparing Himself for His career. His mind was busy grasping the vast proportions of the task before Him. His eyes were looking forth on the country, and His heart smarting with the sense of its sin and shame. In Himself He felt moving the gigantic powers necessary to cope with the vast design; and the desire was gradually growing to an irresistible passion, to go forth and utter the thought within Him, and do the work which had been given Him to do. (John 17:4)

Jesus had only three years to accomplish His life-work. If we remember how quickly three years in an ordinary life pass away, and how little at their close there usually is to show for them, we shall see what must have been the size and quality of that character, and what the unity and intensity of design in that life, which in so marvelously short a time made such a deep and ineffaceable impression on the world, and left to mankind such a heritage of truth and influence.

It is generally allowed that Jesus appeared as a public man with a mind whose ideas were completely developed and arranged, and with designs that marched forward to their ends without hesitation. No deflection took place. The reason of this must have been, that during the thirty years before His public work began, His ideas, His character and designs went through all the stages of a thorough development. Unpretentious as the external aspects of His life at Nazareth were, it was, below the surface, a life of intensity, variety and grandeur. His preparation lasted long. For one with His powers at command, thirty years of complete reticence and reserve were a long time. Nothing was greater in Him afterwards than the majestic reserve in both speech and action which characterized Him. This, too, was learned in Nazareth. There He waited till the hour of the completion of His preparation struck. Nothing could tempt Him forth before the time.

At last, however, He threw down the carpenter's tools, laid aside the workman's dress, and bade His home and the beloved valley of Nazareth farewell. Still, however, all was not ready. His manhood, though it had waxed in secret to such noble proportions, still required a peculiar endowment for the work He had to do; and His ideas and designs, mature as they were, required to be hardened in the fire of a momentous trial. The two final incidents of His preparation—the Baptism and the Temptation—had still to take place.

HIS BAPTISM

Jesus did not descend on the nation from the obscurity of Nazareth without note of warning. His work may be said to have been begun before He Himself put His hand to it—by John the Baptist.

Once more, before hearing the voice of its Messiah, the nation was to hear the long-silent voice of prophecy. The news went through all the country that in the desert of Judea a preacher had appeared,—not like the numbers of dead men's ideas who spoke in the synagogues, or the courtier-like, smooth-tongued teachers of Jerusalem but a rude, strong man, speaking from the heart to the heart, with the authority of one who was sure of his inspiration. He had been a Nazarite from the womb; he had lived for years in the desert, wandering, in communion with his own heart, beside the lonely shores of the Dead Sea; he was clad in the hair cloak and leather girdle of the old prophets; and his ascetic rigor sought no finer fare than locusts and the wild honey which he found in the wilderness. (Mark 1:8)

Yet he knew life well; he was acquainted with all the evils of the time, the hypocrisy of the religious parties, and the corruption of the masses: he had a wonderful power of searching the heart and shaking the conscience, and without fear laid bare the darling sins of every class. But that which most of all attracted attention to him and thrilled every Jewish heart from one end of the land to the other, was the message which he bore— that the Messiah was just at hand, and about to set up the kingdom of God. All Jerusalem poured out to him; the Pharisees were eager to hear the Messianic news; and even the Sadducees were stirred for a moment from their lethargy. The provinces sent forth their thousands to his preaching, and the scattered and hidden ones who longed and prayed for the redemption of Israel flocked to welcome the heart-stirring promise. (Matthew 3:1-12)

But along with it John had another message, which excited very different feelings in different minds. He had to tell his hearers that the nation as a whole was utterly unprepared for the Messiah; that the mere fact of their descent from Abraham would not be a sufficient token of admission to His kingdom; it was to be a kingdom of righteousness and holiness, and Christ's very first work would be to reject all who were not marked with these qualities, as the farmer winnows away the chaff with his fan, and the master of the vineyard hews down every tree that brings forth no fruit. Therefore he called the nation at large—every class and every individual—to repentance, so long as there still was time, as an indispensable preparation for enjoying the blessings of the new epoch; and he baptized in the Jordan all who received his message with faith. Many were stirred with fear and hope and submitted to the rite, but many more were irritated by the exposure of their sins and turned away in anger and unbelief. Among these were the Pharisees, upon whom he was specially severe, and who were deeply offended because he had treated so lightly their descent from Abraham, on which they laid so much stress. (Luke 3:3-9)

One day there appeared among the Baptist's hearers

One who particularly attracted his attention. And when He presented Himself, after the discourse was done, among the candidates for baptism, John drew back, feeling that This was no subject for the bath of repentance, which without hesitation he had administered to all others, and that he himself had no right to baptize Him. It was Jesus, who had come straight hither from the workshop of Nazareth. John and Jesus appear never to have met before, though their families were related and the connection of their careers had been predicted before their birth. But when, in obedience to the injunction of Jesus, John proceeded to administer baptism, he witnessed the sign given by which, as God had instructed him, he was to recognize the Messiah, whose forerunner he was. The Holy Spirit descended on Jesus, as He emerged from the water, and the voice of God pronounced Him in thunder His beloved Son. (Matthew 3:13-17; John 1:29-34)

The baptism itself had an important significance for Jesus —the fulfilment of righteousness. To the other candidates it was related to their old sins, and their entrance into the new Messianic era. To Jesus it could not have the former meaning. But it meant that He too was now entering through this door into the new epoch, of which He was Himself to be the Author. It expressed His sense that the time had come to leave behind the employments of Nazareth and devote himself to His peculiar work.

But still more important was the descent upon Him of the Holy Spirit. This was neither a meaningless display nor merely a signal to the Baptist. It was the special gift then given to qualify Him for His work, and crown the long development of His peculiar powers. We are apt to imagine that His divine nature rendered this unnecessary. On the contrary, His human nature had both to be endowed with the highest gifts and constantly sustained in their exercise. This gift was given Him at baptism. To Him the Holy Spirit was given without measure, while to others was always only in measure. (John 3:34)

THE TEMPTATIONS

Although His preparation for His work had been going on for many years, although His whole heart had long been fixed on it, and His plan had been clearly settled, it was natural that, when the divine signal had been given that it was forthwith to commence, and He felt Himself suddenly put in possession of the supernatural powers necessary for carrying it out, His mind should be in a tumult of crowding thoughts and feelings, and He should seek a place of solitude to resolve once more the whole situation. Accordingly, He hastily retreated from the bank of the Jordan, driven, we are told, by the Spirit, which had just been given Him, into the wilderness, where, for forty days, He wandered among the sandy dunes and wild mountains, His mind being so highly strung with the emotions and ideas which crowded on Him, that He forgot even to eat. (Matthew 4:1-11; Luke 4:1-13)

But it is with surprise and awe we learn that His soul was, during those days, the scene of a frightful struggle. He was tempted of Satan, we are told. What could He be tempted with at a time so sacred? To understand this we must recall what has been said of the state of the

Jewish nation, and especially the nature of the Messianic hopes which they were indulging. They expected a Messiah who would work dazzling wonders and establish a world-wide empire with Jerusalem as its center, and they had postponed the ideas of righteousness and holiness to these. Now what Jesus was tempted to do was, in carrying out the great work which His Father had committed to Him, to yield in some measure to these expectations. He must have foreseen that, unless He did so, the nation would be disappointed and probably turn away from Him in unbelief and anger. (Matthew 20:20, 21; John 8:36)

The suggestion that He should turn stones into bread to satisfy His hunger was a temptation to use the power of working miracles, with which He had just been endowed, for a purpose inferior to those for which alone it had been given.

The suggestion that He should leap from the pinnacle of the temple was probably also a temptation to gratify the vulgar desire for wonders, because it was a part of the popular belief that the Messiah should appear suddenly, and in some marvelous way; as, for instance, by a leap from the temple roof into the midst of the crowds assembled below.

The third and greatest temptation, to win the empire of all the kingdoms of the world by an act of worship to the Evil One, was manifestly a symbol of obedience to the universal Jewish conception of the coming kingdom as a vast structure of material force. It was a temptation which every worker for God, weary with the slow progress of goodness, must often feel, and to which even good and earnest men have sometimes given way—to begin at the outside instead of within, to get first a great shell of external conformity to religion, and afterwards fill it with the reality.

It is with awe we think of these suggestions presenting themselves to the holy soul of Jesus. Could He be tempted to distrust God, and even to worship the Evil One? No doubt the temptations were flung from Him, as the impotent billows retire broken from the breast of the rock on which they have dashed themselves. We must remember that it is no sin to be tempted, it is only sin to yield to temptation. And, indeed, the more absolutely pure a soul is, the more painful will be the point of the temptation, as it presses for admission into his breast. (I Peter 2:22)

Although the tempter only departed from Jesus for a season, this was a decisive struggle; he was thoroughly beaten back, and his power broken at its heart. Jesus emerged from the wilderness with the plan of His life hardened in the fire of trial. Nothing is more conspicuous in His remaining life than the resolution with which He carried it out. Other men, even those who have accomplished the greatest tasks, have sometimes had no definite plan, but only seen by degrees in the evolution of circumstances the path to pursue; their purposes have been modified by events and the advice of others. But Jesus started with His plan perfected, and never deviated from it by a hair's-breadth. And His plan was to establish the kingdom of God in the hearts of individuals, and rely not on the weapons of political and material strength, but only on the power of love and the force of truth. (John 8:36; Luke 17:21)

THE DIVISIONS OF HIS PUBLIC MINISTRY

The public ministry of Jesus is generally reckoned to have lasted three years. Each of them had peculiar features of its own. The first may be called the *Year of Obscurity*, both because the records of it which we possess are very scanty, and because He seems during it to have been only slowly emerging into public notice. It was spent for the most part in Judea. The second was the *Year of Public Favor*, during which the country had become thoroughly aware of Him, His activity was incessant, and His fame rang through the length and breadth of the land. It was almost wholly passed in Galilee. The third was the *Year of Opposition*, when the public favor ebbed away, His enemies multiplied and assailed Him with more and more pertinacity, and at last He fell a victim to their hatred. The first six months of this final year were passed in Galilee, and the last six in other parts of the land. (It is widely accepted that the *Year of Obscurity* did not last a full twelve months and probably lasted no more than four to six months; the *Year of Public Favor*, spent largely in Galilee, lasted about eighteen months; the *Year of Opposition* consumed most of the last twelve months of Jesus' ministry, and were spent chiefly in Judea and Peræa. The author's use of the word *Year* should be interpreted in a loose way rather than to mean an exact period of twelve months.—the Editors)

Thus the life of the Savior in its external outline resembled that of many a reformer and benefactor of mankind. Such a life often begins with a period during which the public is gradually made aware of the new man in its midst, then passes into a period when his doctrine or reform is borne aloft on the shoulders of popularity, and ends with a reaction, when the old prejudices and interests which have been assailed by him rally from his attack, and, gaining to themselves the passions of the crowd, crush him in their rage.

FIVE

The Year of Obscurity

The records of this year which we possess are extremely meager, comprising only two or three incidents, which may be here enumerated, especially as they form a kind of program of His future work.

When He emerged from the wilderness after the forty days of temptation, with His grasp of His future plan tightened by that awful struggle, He appeared once more on the bank of the Jordan, and John pointed Him out as the great Successor to himself of whom he had often spoken. He especially introduced Him to some of the choisest of His own disciples, who immediately became His followers. Probably the very first of these to whom He spoke was the man who was afterwards to be His favorite disciple, and to give to the world the divinest portrait of His character and life—John the Evangelist. The other young men who attached themselves to Him at the same time were Andrew, Peter, Philip, and Nathanael. They had been prepared for their new Master by their association with the Baptist, and although they did not at once give up their employments and follow Him in the same way as they did at a later period, they received impressions at their very first meeting which decided their whole after-career. (John 1:29-49)

The Baptist's disciples do not seem to have at once gone over in a body to Christ. But the best of them did so. However, some mischief-makers endeavored to excite envy in his mind by pointing out how his influence was passing away to Another. But they little understood that great man, whose chief greatness was his humility. He answered them that it was his joy to decrease, while Christ increased, for it was Christ who as the Bridegroom was to lead home the bride, while he was only the Bridegroom's friend, whose happiness consisted in seeing the crown of festal joy placed on the head of another. (John 3:25-30)

HIS FIRST MIRACLE

With His newly attached followers Jesus departed from the scene of John's ministry, and went north to Cana in Galilee, to attend a marriage to which He had been invited. Here He made the first display of the miraculous powers with which He had been recently endowed, by turning water into wine. It was a manifestation of His glory intended specially for his new disciples, who, we are told, thenceforward believed on Him, which means, no doubt, that they were fully convinced that He was the Messiah. It was intended also to strike the keynote of His ministry, showing that He was to mingle in their common life, and produce a happy revolution in their circumstances, which would be like the turning of the water of their life into wine. (John 2:1-11)

HE CLEANSED THE TEMPLE

Soon after this miracle He returned again to Judea to attend the Passover, and gave a still more striking proof of the joyful and enthusiastic mood in which He was then living, by purging the temple of the sellers of animals and the money-changers, who had introduced their traffic into its courts. These persons were allowed to carry on their sacrilegious trade under the pretence of accommodating strangers who came to worship at Jerusalem, by selling them the victims which they could not bring from foreign countries, and supplying, in exchange for foreign money, the Jewish coins in which alone they could pay their temple dues. But what had been begun under the veil of a pious pretext had ended in gross commercialism. Jesus had probably often witnessed the disgraceful scene with indignation during His visits to Jerusalem, and now He drove out the money changers and overthrew their tables. It was the beginning of His reformatory work against the religious abuses of the time. (John 2:13-25)

KINGDOM EXPLAINED TO NICODEMUS

He wrought other miracles during the feast, which must have excited much talk among the pilgrims from every land who crowded the city. One result of them was to bring to His lodging one night the venerable and anxious inquirer to whom He delivered the marvelous discourse on the nature of the new kingdom He had come to found, and the grounds of admission to it, which has been preserved to us in the third chapter of John. It seemed a hopeful sign that one of the heads of the nation should approach Him in a spirit so humble; but Nicode-

mus was the only one of them on whose mind the first
display of the Messiah's power in the capital produced a
deep and favorable impression. (John 3:1-7)

REASONS FOR THE MEAGER RECORDS

Thus far we follow clearly the first steps of Jesus.
But at this point our information in regard to the first
year of His ministry, after commencing with such fulness, comes to a sudden stop, and for the next eight
months, we learn nothing more about Him but that He
was baptizing in Judea—"though Jesus Himself baptized not, but His disciples"—and that He "made and
baptized more disciples than John." (John 4:1-3)

What can be the meaning of such a blank? It is to be
noted, too, that it is only in the Fourth Gospel that we
receive even the details given above. The Synoptists omit
the first year of the ministry altogether, beginning their
narrative with the ministry in Galilee, and merely indi-
cating in the most cursory way that there was a ministry
in Judea before.

We shall perhaps be conducted to the explanation by
attending to the little-noticed fact, which John communi-
cates, that for a time Jesus took up the work of the Baptist. He baptized by the hands of His disciples, and drew
even larger crowds than John. Must not this mean that
He was convinced, by the small impression which His
manifestation of Himself at the Passover had made, that
the nation was utterly unprepared for receiving Him yet
as the Messiah, and that what was needed was the exten-
sion of the preparatory work of repentance and baptism,
and accordingly, keeping in the background His higher
character, became for the time the colleague of John?

This view is confirmed by the fact, that it was upon John's imprisonment at this year's end that He opened fully His Messianic career in Galilee. (Matthew 4:12)

A still deeper explanation of the silence of the Synoptists over this period, and their scant notice of Christ's subsequent visits to Jerusalem, has been suggested that He was gathering the company of believing souls that was to form the nucleus of His church.

SIX

The Year of Public Favor —
The Scene of This Year's Work

After the year spent in the south, Jesus shifted the sphere of His activity to the north of the country. In Galilee He would be able to address Himself to minds that were unsophisticated with the prejudices and super-cilious pride of Judea, where the sacerdotal and learned classes had their headquarters; and He might hope that, if His doctrine and influence took a deep hold of one part of the country, even though it was remote from the cen-ter of authority, He might return to the south backed with an irresistible national acknowledgment, and carry by storm even the citadel of prejudice itself.

GALILEE

The area of His activity for the next eighteen months was very limited. Even the whole of Palestine was a very limited country. It is important to remember this, be-cause it renders intelligible the rapidity with which the movement of Jesus spread over the land, and all parts of the country flocked to His ministry; and it is interesting to remember it as an illustration of the fact, that the nations which have contributed most to the civilization of the world have, during the period of their true greatness, been confined to very small territories. Rome was but a single city, and Greece a very small country.

Galilee was the most northerly of the four provinces into which Palestine was divided. It was sixty miles long by thirty broad. It consisted for the most part of an elevated plateau, whose surface was varied by irregular mountain masses. Near its eastern boundary it suddenly dropped down into a great gulf, through which flowed the Jordan, and in the midst of which, at a depth of five hundred feet below the Mediterranean, lay the lovely, harp-shaped Sea of Galilee. The whole province was very fertile, and its surface thickly covered with large villages and towns.

But the center of activity was the basin of the lake, a sheet of water thirteen miles long by six broad. Above its eastern shore, round which ran a fringe of green a quarter of a mile broad, there towered high, bare hills, cloven with the channels of torrents. On the western side, the mountains were gently sloped and their sides richly cultivated, bearing splendid crops of every description; while at their feet the shore was verdant with luxuriant groves of olives, oranges, figs, and every product of an almost tropical climate.

At the northern end of the lake the space between the water and the mountains was broadened by the delta of the river, and watered with many streams from the hills, so that it was a perfect paradise of fertility and beauty. It was called the plain of Gennesareth, and even at this day, when the whole basin of the lake is little better than a torrid solitude, is still covered with magnificent cornfields, wherever the hand of cultivation touches it; and, where idleness leaves it untended, is overspread with thick jungles of thorn and oleander. In our Lord's time, it contained the chief cities on the lake, such as Capernaum, Bethsaida, and Chorazin. But the whole shore was studded with towns and villages, and formed a perfect beehive of swarming human life. The means of existence were abundant in the crops and fruits of every description which the fields yielded so richly; and the waters of the lake teemed with fish, affording employment to thousands of fishermen.

Besides, the great highways from Egypt to Damascus, and from Phœnicia to the Euphrates, passed here, and made this a vast center of traffic. Thousands of boats for fishing, transport, and pleasure moved to and fro on the surface of the lake, so that the whole region was a focus of energy and prosperity.

The report of the miracles which Jesus had wrought at Jerusalem, eight months before, had been brought home to Galilee by the pilgrims who had been south at the feast, and doubtless also the news of His preaching and baptism in Judea had created talk and excitement before He arrived. Accordingly, the Galileans were in some measure prepared to receive Him when He returned to their midst.

VISITED THE HOME OF HIS YOUTH

One of the first places He visited was Nazareth, the home of His childhood and youth. He appeared there one Sabbath in the synagogue, and was invited to read the Scriptures and address the congregation. He read a passage in Isaiah, in which a glowing description is given of the coming and work of the Messiah: "The Spirit of the

Lord God is upon me, because He has anointed me to preach the gospel to the poor; He hath sent me to heal the broken-hearted, to preach deliverance to the captives, and recovering of sight to the blind, to set at liberty them that are bruised, to preach the acceptable year of the Lord." As He commented on this text, picturing the features of the Messianic time,—the emancipation of the slave, the enriching of the poor, the healing of the diseased,—their curiosity at hearing for the first time a young preacher who had been brought up among themselves passed into spell-bound wonder, and they burst into the applause which used to be allowed in the Jewish synagogues. (Luke 4:16-20; Isaiah 61:1)

But soon the reaction came. They began to whisper: Was not this the carpenter who had worked among them? Had not His father and mother been their neighbors? Were not His sisters married in the town? Their envy was excited. And when He proceeded to tell them that the prophecy which He had read was fulfilled in Himself, they broke out into angry scorn. They demanded of Him a sign, such as it was reported He had given in Jerusalem; and when He informed them that He could do no miracle among the unbelieving, they rushed on Him in a storm of jealousy and wrath, and hurrying Him out of the synagogue to a crag behind the town, would, if He had not miraculously taken Himself away from them, have flung Him over, and crowned their proverbial wickedness with a deed which would have robbed Jerusalem of her bad eminence of being the murderess of the Messiah. (Luke 4:20-29)

MADE CAPERNAUM HIS HOME

From that day Nazareth was His home no more. Once

again, indeed, in His yearning love for His old neighbors, He visited it, but with no better result. Henceforward He made His home in Capernaum, on the northwestern shore of the Sea of Galilee. This town has completely vanished out of existence; its very site can not now be discovered with any certainty. This may be one reason why it is not connected in the Christian mind with the life of Jesus in the same prominent way as Bethlehem, where He was born, Nazareth, where He was brought up, and Jerusalem, where He died. But we ought to fix it in our memories side by side with these, for it was His home for eighteen of the most important months of His life. It is called His own city, and He was asked for tribute in it as a citizen of the place. It was thoroughly well adapted to be the center of His labors in Galilee, for it was the focus of the busy life in the basin of the lake, and was conveniently situated for excursions to all parts of the province. Whatever happened there was quickly heard of in all the regions round about. (Luke 4:30,31; Matthew 17:24-27)

In Capernaum, then, He began His Galilean work; and for many months the method of His life was, to be frequently there as in His headquarters, and from this center to make tours in all directions, visiting the towns and villages of Galilee. Sometimes His journey would be inland, away to the west. At other times it would be a tour of the villages on the lake, or a visit to the country on its eastern side. He had a boat that waited on Him, to convey Him wherever He might wish to go. He would come back to Capernaum, perhaps only for a day, perhaps for a week or two at a time.

In a few weeks the whole province was ringing with His name; He was the subject of conversation in every boat on the lake and every house in the whole region; men's minds were stirred with the profoundest excitement, and everyone desired to see Him. Crowds began to gather about Him. They grew larger and larger. They multiplied to thousands and tens of thousands. They followed Him wherever He went. The news spread far and wide beyond Galilee, and brought hosts from Jerusalem, Judea, and Peræa, and even from Idumæa in the far south, and Tyre and Sidon in the far north. Sometimes He could not stay in any town, because the crowds blocked up the streets and trode one on another. He had to take them out to the fields and deserts. The country was stirred from end to end, and Galilee was all on fire with excitement about Him. (Luke 4:37; 5:1-3, 15-17)

SEVEN

The Year of Public Favor —
The Means He Employed

The two great means which Jesus used in His work, and which created such attention and enthusiasm, were His Miracles and His Teaching.

THE MIRACLE-WORKER

Perhaps His miracles excited the widest attention. We are told how the news of the first one which He wrought in Capernaum spread like wildfire through the town, and brought crowds about the house where He was; and whenever He performed a new one of extraordinary character, the excitement grew intense and the rumor of it spread on every hand. When, for instance, He first cured leprosy, the most malignant form of bodily disease in Palestine, the amazement of the people knew no bounds. It was the same when He first overcame a case of possession; and when he raised to life the widow's son at Nain, there ensued a sort of stupor of fear, followed by delighted wonder and the talk of thousands of tongues. (Luke 4:31-37; 5:12-16; 7:11-17; Mark 1:21-45)

All Galilee was for a time in motion with the crowding of the diseased of every description who could walk or totter to be near Him, and with companies of anxious friends carrying on beds and couches those who could not come themselves. The streets of the villages and towns were lined with the victims of disease as His benignant figure passed by. Sometimes He had so many to attend to that He could not find time even to eat; and at one period He was so absorbed in His benevolent labors, and so carried along with the holy excitement which they caused, that His relatives, with indecorous rashness, endeavored to interfere, saying to each other that He was beside Himself. (Luke 4:40; 5:19-24; Mark 3:20, 21; 6:53-56)

The miracles of Jesus, taken altogether, were of two classes—those wrought on man, and those wrought in the sphere of external nature, such as the turning of water into wine, stilling the tempest, and multiplying the loaves. The former were by far the more numerous. They consisted chiefly of cures of diseases less or more malignant, such as lameness, blindness, deafness, palsy, leprosy, and so forth. He appears to have varied very much His mode of acting, for reasons which we can scarcely explain. Sometimes He used means, such as a touch, or the laying of moistened clay on the part, or ordering the patient to wash in water. At other times He healed without any means, and occasionally even at a distance. Besides these bodily cures, He dealt with the diseases of the mind. These seem to have been peculiarly prevalent in Palestine at the time, and to have excited the utmost terror. They were believed to be accompanied by the entrance of demons into the poor imbecile or raving victims, and this idea was only too true. The man whom Jesus cured among the tombs in the country of the Gadarenes was a frightful example of this class of disease; and the picture of him sitting at the feet of Jesus, clothed and in his right mind, shows what an effect His kind, soothing, and authoritative presence had on minds so distracted. But the most extraordinary of the miracles of Jesus upon man were the instances in which He raised the dead to life. They were not frequent, but naturally produced an overwhelming impression whenever they occurred. (Luke 7:11-15; 11:33-45)

The miracles of the other class—those on external nature—were of the same inexplicable description. Some of His cures of mental disease, if standing by themselves, might be accounted for by the influence of a powerful nature on a troubled mind; and in the same way some of His bodily cures might be accounted for by His influencing the body through the mind. But such a miracle as walking on the tempestuous sea is utterly beyond the reach of natural explanation. (Matthew 14:25)

Why did Jesus employ this means of working? Several answers may be given to this question.

First, He wrought miracles because His Father gave Him these signs as proofs that He had sent Him. It was a stupendous claim which He made on the faith of men when He announced Himself as the Messiah, and it would have been unreasonable to expect it to be conceded by a nation accustomed to miracles as the signs of a divine mission, if He had wrought none. (John 3:2; 10: 25, 37, 38; 11:45; 20:30,31)

Secondly, the miracles of Christ were the natural outflow of the divine fulness which dwelt in Him. God was in Him, and His human nature was endowed with the

Holy Spirit without measure. It was natural, when such a Being was in the world, that mighty works should manifest themselves in Him. He was Himself the great miracle, of which His particular miracles were merely sparks or emanations. Therefore all His miracles bore the stamp of His character. They were not mere exhibitions of power, but also of holiness, wisdom, and love. The Jews often sought from Him mere gigantesque prodigies, to gratify their mania for marvels. But He always refused them, working only such miracles as were helps to faith. They were marked by unvarying sobriety and benevolence, because they were the expressions of His character as a whole.

Thirdly, His miracles were symbols of His spiritual and saving work. You have only to consider them for a moment to see that they were, as a whole, triumphs over the misery of the world. Mankind is the prey of a thousand evils, and even the frame of external nature bears the mark of some past catastrophe: "The whole creation groaneth and travaileth in pain." This huge mass of physical evil in the lot of mankind is the effect of sin. Not that every disease and misfortune can be traced to special sin, although some of them can. The consequences of past sin are distributed in detail over the whole race. But yet the misery of the world is the shadow of its sin. Material and moral evil, being thus intimately related, mutually illustrate each other. When He healed bodily blindness, it was a type of the healing of the inner eye; when He raised the dead, He meant to suggest that He was the Resurrection and the Life in the spiritual world as well; when He cleansed the leper, His triumph spoke of another over the leprosy of sin; when He multiplied the loaves, He followed the miracle with a discourse on the bread of life; when He stilled the storm, it was an assurance that He could speak peace to the troubled conscience. (Romans 8:22)

Thus His miracles were a natural and essential part of His Messianic work. They were an excellent means of making Him known to the nation.

THE TEACHER

The other great instrument with which Jesus did His work was His teaching. It was by far the more important of the two. His miracles were only the bell tolled to bring the people to hear His words.

The miracles probably made most noise, but His preaching also spread His fame far and wide. There is no power whose attraction is more unfailing than that of the eloquent word. Barbarians, listening to their bards and story-tellers; Greeks, listening to the restrained passion of their orators, and matter-of-fact nations like the Roman, have alike acknowledged its power to be irresistible. The Jews prized it above almost every other attraction, and among the figures of their mighty dead revered none more highly than the prophets—those eloquent utterers of the truth, whom Heaven had sent them from age to age.

Jesus also was recognized as a prophet, and accordingly, His preaching created wide-spread excitement. "He spake in their synagogues, being glorified of all." His words were heard with wonder and amazement. Sometimes the multitude on the beach of the lake so pressed upon Him to hear, that He had to enter into a ship and address them from the deck, as they spread themselves out in a semicircle on the ascending shore.

A good shepherd tenderly cares for his sheep.

His enemies themselves bore witness that "never man spake like this man"; and meager as are the remains of His preaching which we possess, they are amply sufficient to make us echo the sentiment and understand the impression which He produced. All His words together which have been preserved to us would not occupy more space in print than half-a-dozen ordinary sermons; yet it is not too much to say, that they are the most precious literary heritage of the human race. His words, like His miracles, were expressions of Himself, and every one of them has in it something of the grandeur of His character. (Luke 5:1-3; John 6:63; 7:46)

The form of the preaching of Jesus was essentially Jewish. It consisted of numerous sayings, every one of which contained the greatest possible amount of truth in the smallest possible compass, and was expressed in language so concise and pointed as to stick in the memory like an arrow. Read them, and you will find that every one of them, as you ponder it, sucks the mind in and in like a whirlpool, till it is lost in the depths.

But there was another characteristic of the form of Jesus' teaching. It was full of figures of speech. He thought in images. He had ever been a loving and accurate observer of nature around Him—of the colors of the flowers, the ways of the birds, the growth of the trees, the vicissitudes of the seasons—and an equally keen observer of the ways of men in all parts of life— in religion, in business, in the home. The result was that He could neither think nor speak without His thought running into the mould of some natural image. His preaching was alive with such references, and therefore full of color, movement, and changing forms. There were no abstract statements in it; they were all changed into pictures.

Thus, in His sayings, we can still see the aspects of the country and the life of the time as in a panorama— the lilies, whose gorgeous beauty His eyes feasted on, waving in the fields; the sheep following the shepherd; the broad and narrow city gates; the virgins with their lamps awaiting in the darkness the bridal procession; the Pharisee with his broad phylacteries and the publican with bent head at prayer together in the temple; the rich man seated in his palace at a feast, and the beggar lying at his gate with the dogs licking his sores; and a hundred other pictures that lay bare the inner and minute life of the time, over which history in general sweeps heedlessly with majestic stride.

But the most characteristic form of speech He made use of was the parable. It was a combination of the two qualities already mentioned—concise, memorable expression, and a figurative style. It used an incident, taken from common life and rounded into a gem-like picture, to set forth some corresponding truth in the higher and spiritual region. It was a favorite Jewish mode of putting truth, but Jesus imparted to it by far the richest and most perfect development. About one-third of all His sayings which have been preserved to us consists of parables. (Matthew 13:3,34)

The hearers of the sermons of any preacher will probably, after a few years, remember the illustrations they have contained far better than anything else in them. How these parables have remained in the memory of all generations since! The Prodigal Son, the Sower, the Ten Virgins, the Good Samaritan,—these and many others are pictures hung up in millions of minds.

Jesus took the commonest objects and incidents around Him,—the sewing of a piece of cloth on an old garment, the bursting of an old bottle, the children playing in the market-place at weddings and funerals, or the tumbling of a hut in a storm,—to change them into perfect pictures, and to make them the vehicles for conveying to the world immortal truth. No wonder the crowds followed Him! There never was speaking so simple yet so profound, so pictorial yet so absolutely true. (Mark 12:37)

Such were the qualities of His style. *The qualities of the Preacher Himself have been preserved to us in the criticism of His hearers*, and are manifest in the remains of His addresses which the Gospels contain.

The most prominent of them seems to have been *Authority*: "The people were astonished at His doctrine, for He taught them as one having authority, and not as the scribes." The first thing His hearers were struck with was the contrast between His words and the preaching which they were wont to hear from the scribes in the synagogues. These were the exponents of the deadest and driest system of theology that has ever passed in any age for religion. Instead of expounding the Scriptures, which were in their hands, and would have lent living power to their words, they retailed the opinions of commentators, and were afraid to advance any statement, unless it was backed by the authority of some master. Instead of dwelling on the great themes of justice and mercy, love and God, they tortured the sacred text into a ceremonial manual, and preached on the proper breadth of phylacteries, the proper postures for prayer, the proper length of fasts, and so forth; for in these things the religion of the time consisted. (Matthew 7:28,29; 23:5,23)

Jesus knew nothing of the authority of masters and schools of interpretation, but spoke as One whose own eyes had gazed on the objects of the eternal world. He needed none to tell Him of God or of man, for He knew both perfectly. He was possessed with the sense of a mission, which drove Him on and imparted earnestness to every word and gesture. He knew Himself sent from God, and the words He spoke to be not His own, but God's. He warned them that on their acceptance or rejection of the message He bore would depend their future weal or woe. This was the tone of earnestness, of majesty and authority that smote His hearers with awe. (John 8:26; 13:3; 12:48)

Another quality which the people remarked in Him was *Boldness*: "Lo, He speaketh boldly." The preacher who is afraid of his audience, and respects the persons of the learned and the great, is thinking of himself and of what will be said of his performance. But he who feels himself driven on by a divine mission forgets himself. All audiences are alike to him, be they gentle or simple; he is thinking only of the message he has to deliver. Jesus was ever looking the spiritual and eternal realities in the face; the spell of their greatness held Him, and all human distinctions disappeared in their presence; men of every class were only men to Him. (John 7:26)

He discovered His boldness chiefly in attacking the abuses and ideals of the time. It would be a complete mistake to think of Him as all mildness and meekness. There is scarcely any element more conspicuous in His words than a strain of fierce indignation. It was an age of shams above almost any that have ever been. They occupied all high places. They paraded themselves in social life, occupied the chairs of learning, and above all debased every part of religion. One can feel throbbing through His words, from first to last, an indignation against all this, which had begun with His earliest observation in Nazareth and ripened with His increasing knowledge of the times. The things which were highly esteemed among men, He broadly asserted, were abomination in the sight of God. There never was in the history of speech a polemic so scathing, so annihilating, as His against the figures to which the reverence of the multitude had been paid before His withering words fell on them — the scribe, the Pharisee, the priest, and the Levite. (Matthew 23)

A third quality which His hearers remarked was *Power*: "His word was with power." He was filled with the Spirit without measure. Therefore the truth possessed Him. It burned and swelled in His own bosom, and He spoke it forth from heart to heart. (Luke 4:32)

A fourth quality which was observed in His preaching, and was surely a very prominent one, was *Graciousness*: "They wondered at the gracious words which proceeded out of His mouth." In spite of His tone of authority and His fearless and scathing attacks on the times, there was diffused over all He said a glow of grace and love. Here especially His character spoke. The scribes of the time were hard, proud, and loveless. They flattered the rich and honored the learned. But to Jesus every soul was infinitely precious. Therefore He spoke to His hearers of every grade with the same respect. Surely it was the divine love itself, uttering itself from the innermost recess of the divine being, that spoke in the parables of the fifteenth of Luke. (Luke 4:22)

Such were some of the qualities of the Preacher. And one more may be mentioned, which may be said to embrace all the rest, and is perhaps the highest quality of public speech. *He addressed men as men, not as members of any class or possessors of any peculiar culture.* The differences which divide men, such as wealth, rank, and education, are on the surface. The elements in which they are all alike — the broad sense of the understanding, the great passions of the heart, the primary instincts of the conscience — are profound. Not that these are the same in all men. In some they are deeper, in others shallower; but in all they are far deeper than aught else. He who addresses them appeals to the deepest thing in His hearers. He will be equally intelligible to all. Every hearer will receive his own portion from Him; the small and shallow mind will get as much as it can take, and the largest and deepest will get its fill at the same feast. This is why the words of Jesus are perennial in their freshness. They are for all generations, and equally for all. (Mark 16:15,16)

When we come to inquire what the matter of Jesus' preaching consisted of, we perhaps naturally expect to find Him expounding the system of doctrine which we are ourselves acquainted with, in the forms, say, of the Catechism, Confession of Faith, or Church Manual, or even unwritten creeds. But what we find is very different. He did not make use of any system of doctrine. He did not use theological phraseology. But He spoke in the language of life, and concentrated His preaching on a few burning points, that touched the heart, the conscience and the time.

The central idea and the commonest phrase of His preaching was "the kingdom of God." It will be remembered how many of His parables begin with "The kingdom of Heaven is like," so and so. He said, "I must preach the kingdom of God to other cities also," thereby characterizing the matter of His preaching; and in the same way He is said to have sent forth the apostles "to preach the kingdom of God." He did not invent the phrase. It was a historical one handed down from the past, and was common in the mouths of His contemporaries. The Baptist had made large use of it, the burden of his message being, "The kingdom of God is at hand." (Matthew 13:24; Mark 1:15; Luke 4:43)

What did it signify? It meant the new era, which the prophets had predicted and the saints had looked for. Jesus announced that it had come, and that He had brought it. The time of waiting was fulfilled. Many prophets and righteous men, He told His contemporaries, had desired to see the things which they saw, but had not seen them. He declared that so great were the privileges and glories of the new time, that the least partaker of them was greater than the Baptist, though he had been the greatest representative of the old time. (Matthew 13:17; 11:11)

All this was no more than His contemporaries would have expected to hear, if they had recognized that the kingdom of God was really come. But they looked round, and asked where the new era was which Jesus said He had brought. Here He and they were at complete variance. They emphasized the first part of the phrase, "the kingdom," He the second, "of God." They expected the new era to appear in magnificent material forms,—in a kingdom of which God indeed was to be the ruler, but which was to show itself in worldly splendor, in force of arms, in a universal empire. Jesus saw the new era in an empire of God over the loving heart and the obedient will. They looked for it outside. He said, "It is within you." They looked for a period of external glory and happiness. He placed the glory and blessedness of the new time in character. (Luke 17:21)

So He began His Sermon on the Mount, that great manifesto of the new era, with a series of "Blesseds." But the blessedness was entirely that of character. And it was a character totally different from that which was then looked up to as imparting glory and happiness to its possessor—that of the proud Pharisee, the wealthy Sadducee, or the learned scribe. Blessed, said He, are the poor in spirit, they that mourn, the meek, they which do hunger and thirst after righteousness, the merciful, the pure in heart, the peacemakers, they which are persecuted for righteousness' sake. (Matthew 5:1-12)

The main drift of His preaching was to set forth this conception of the kingdom of God, the character of its members, their blessedness in the love and communion of their Father in heaven, and their prospects in the glory of the future world. He exhibited the contrast between it and the formal religion of the time, with its lack of spirituality and its substitution of ceremonial observances for character.

But the center and soul of His preaching was Himself. He contained within Himself the new era. He not only announced it, but created it. The new character which made men subjects of the kingdom and sharers of its privileges was to be got from Him alone. Therefore the practical issue of every address of Christ was the command to come to Him, to learn of Him, to follow Him. "Come unto me, all ye that labor and are heavy laden," was the key-note, the deepest and final word of all His discourses. (Matthew 11:28-30)

The audience of Jesus varied exceedingly both in size and character on different occasions. Very frequently it was the great multitude. He addressed them everywhere —on the mountain, on the sea-shore, on the highway, in the synagogues, in the temple courts. But He was quite as willing to speak with a single individual, however humble. He seized every opportunity of doing so. Although He was worn-out with fatigue, He talked to the woman at the well; He received Nicodemus alone; He taught Mary in her home. There are said to be nineteen such private interviews mentioned in the Gospels. They leave to His followers a memorable example. This is perhaps the most effective of all forms of instruction, as it is certainly the best test of earnestness. A man who preaches to thousands with enthusiasm may be a mere orator, but the man who seeks the opportunity of speaking closely of the welfare of their souls to individuals must have a real fire from heaven burning in his heart. (John 4:5-26; 3:1-21; Luke 10:38-42)

Often His audience consisted of the circle of His disciples. His preaching divided His hearers. He has Himself, in such parables as the Sower, the Tares and the Wheat, the Wedding Feast, and so forth, described with unequalled vividness its effects on different classes. Some it utterly repelled; others heard it with wonder, without being touched in the heart; others were affected for a time, but soon returned to their old interests. It is terrible to think how few there were, even when the Son of God was preaching, who heard unto salvation. Those who did so, gradually formed round Him a body of disciples. They followed Him about, hearing all his discourses, and often He spoke to them alone. Such were the five hundred to whom He appeared in Galilee after His resurrection. Some of them were women, such as Mary Magdalene, Susanna, and Joanna the wife of Herod's steward, who, being wealthy, gladly supplied His few simple wants. To these disciples He gave a more thorough instruction than to the crowd. These became the nucleus of that spiritual society, elevated above all local limitations and distinctions of rank and nationality, in which the spirit and doctrine of Christ were to be spread and perpetuated in the world. (Matthew 22:14)

THE APOSTOLATE

Perhaps the formation of the Apostolate ought to be placed side by side with miracles and preaching as a third means by which He did His work. The men who became the twelve apostles were at first only ordinary disciples like many others. This, at least, was the position of such of them as were already His followers during the first year of His ministry. At the opening of His Galilean activity, their attachment to Him entered on a second stage; He called them to give up their ordinary employments and be with Him constantly. And probably not many weeks afterwards, He promoted them to the third and final stage of nearness to Himself, by ordaining them to be apostles.

It was when His work grew so extensive and pressing

that it was quite impossible for Him to overtake it all, that He multiplied Himself, so to speak, by appointing them His assistants. He commissioned them to teach the simpler elements of His doctrine. In this way many towns were evangelized which He had not time to visit. But, as future events proved, His aims in their appointment were much more far-reaching. His work was for all time and for the whole world. It could not be accomplished in a single lifetime. He foresaw this, and made provision for it by the early choice of agents who might take up His plans after He was gone, and in whom He might still extend His influence over mankind. (Mark 3:14-19)

It is surprising to see what sort of persons He selected for so grand a destiny. They did not belong to the influential and learned classes. No doubt the heads and leaders of the nation ought to have been the organs of their Messiah, but they proved themselves totally unworthy of the great vocation. He was able to do without them; He needed not the influence of carnal power and wisdom. He did not scruple to commit His cause to twelve simple men, destitute of learning and belonging to the common people. He made the selection after a night spent in prayer, and doubtless after many days of deliberation. The event showed with what insight into character He had acted. They turned out to be instruments thoroughly fitted for the great design; and the selection of agents who were at first so unlikely, but in the end proved so successful, will always be one of the chief monuments of the incomparable originality of Jesus.

It would, however, be a very inadequate account of His relation to the Twelve merely to point out the insight with which He discerned in them the germs of fitness for their grand future. They became very great men, and in the founding of the church achieved a work of immeasurable importance. They may be said, in a sense they little dreamed of, to sit on thrones ruling the modern world. They stand like a row of noble pillars towering far across the flats of time. But the sunlight that shines on them, and makes them visible, comes entirely from Him. He gave them all their greatness; and theirs is one of the most striking evidences of His. What must He have been whose influence imparted to them such magnitude of character, and made them fit for so gigantic a task! At first they were rude and carnal in the extreme. What hope was there that they would ever be able to appreciate the designs of a mind like His, to inherit His work, to possess in any degree a spirit so exquisite, and transmit to future generations a faithful image of His character? But he educated them with the most affectionate patience, bearing with their vulgar hopes and their clumsy misunderstandings of His meaning. Never forgetting for a moment the part they were to play in the future, He made their training His most constant work. They were often His only audience, and then He unveiled to them the glories and mysteries of His doctrine, sowing in their minds the seeds of truth which time and experience were by and by to fructify. (Matthew 19:28)

But the most important part of their training was one which was perhaps at the time little noticed, though it was producing splendid results,—the silent and constant influence of His character on theirs. He drew them to Himself and stamped His own image on them. It was this which made them the men they became.

EIGHT

The Year of Public Favor —
The Character of Jesus

HIS HUMAN CHARACTER

His illustrious character consisted of many marvelous traits, which continue to give inspiration and direction to mankind.

Perhaps the most obvious feature which they would remark in Him was *Purposefulness.* This certainly is the ground-tone which sounds in all His sayings which have been preserved to us, and the pulse which we feel beating in all His recorded actions. He was possessed with a purpose which guided and drove Him on. Most lives aim at nothing in particular, but drift along, under the influence of varying moods and instincts or on the currents of society, and achieve nothing. But Jesus evidently had a definite object before Him, which absorbed His thoughts and drew out His energies. He would often give as a reason for not doing something, "Mine hour is not yet come," as if His design absorbed every moment, and every hour had its own allotted part of the task.

This imparted an earnestness and rapidity of execution to His life which most lives altogether lack. (John 2:4)

Very closely connected with this quality was another prominent one, which may be called *Faith,* and by which is meant His astonishing confidence in the accomplishment of His purpose, and apparent disregard both of means and opposition. If it be considered in the most general way how vast His aim was—to reform His nation and begin an everlasting and world-wide religious movement; if the opposition which He encountered, and foresaw His cause would have to meet at every stage of its progress, be considered—His quiet and unwavering confidence in His success will appear only less remarkable than His success itself. This was the simplicity of faith, which does not contrive and prepare, but simply goes onward and does the work. It was the quality which He said could remove mountains, and which He chiefly desiderated in His followers. (John 18:37; Mark 11: 22-24)

A third prominent feature of His character was *Originality.* Most lives are easily explained. They are mere products of circumstances, and copies of thousands like them which surround or have preceded them. The habits and customs of the country to which we belong, the fashion and tastes of our generation, the traditions of our education, the prejudices of our class, the opinions of our school or sect,—these form us.

But what circumstances made the Man Christ Jesus? There never was an age more dry and barren than that in which He was born. He was like a tall, fresh palm springing out of a desert. What was there in the petty life of Nazareth to produce so gigantic a character? How could the notoriously wicked village send forth such breathing purity? It may have been that a scribe taught Him the vocables and grammar of knowledge, but His doctrine was a complete contradiction of all that the scribes taught. The fashions of the sects never laid hold of His free spirit. How clearly, amidst the sounds which filled the ears of His time, He heard the neglected voice of truth, which was quite different from them! How clearly, behind all the pretentious and accepted forms of piety, He saw the lovely and neglected figure of real godliness! He can not be explained by anything which was in the world and might have produced Him. He grew from within. He directed His eyes straight on the facts of nature and life and believed what He saw, instead of allowing His vision to be tutored by what others had said they saw. He was equally loyal to the truth in His words. He went forth and spoke out without hesitation what He believed, though it shook to their foundations the institutions, the creeds, and customs of His country, and loosened the opinions of the populace in a hundred points in which they had been educated. (Matthew 5:21-44)

A fourth and very glorious feature of His character was *Love to Men*. It has been already said that He was possessed with an overmastering purpose. But beneath a great life-purpose there must be a great passion, which shapes and sustains it. Love to men was the passion which directed and inspired Him. It overleapt all the limits which other men have put to their benevolence. Differences of class and nationality usually cool men's interest in each other; in nearly all countries it has been considered a virtue to hate enemies; and it is generally agreed to loathe and avoid those who have outraged the laws of respectability. But He paid no heed to these conventions; the overpowering sense of the preciousness which He perceived in enemy, foreigner, and outcast alike, forbidding Him. This marvelous love shaped the purpose of His life. It gave Him the most tender and intense sympathy with every form of pain and misery. Wherever help was needed, thither His merciful heart drew Him. (John 15:13)

But it was especially to save the soul that His love impelled Him. He knew this was the real jewel, which everything should be done to rescue, and that its miseries and perils were the most dangerous of all. There has sometimes been love to others without this vital aim. But His love was directed by wisdom to the truest weal of those He loved. He knew He was doing His very best for them when He was saving them from their sins. (Romans 5:8; Mark 8:36,37)

But the crowning attribute of His human character was *Love to God*. It is the supreme honor and attainment of man to be one with God in feeling, thought, and purpose. Jesus had this in perfection. To us it is very difficult to realize God. The mass of men scarcely think about Him at all. With Jesus it was not so. He realized God always. He never spent an hour, He never did an action, without direct reference to Him. God was about Him like the atmosphere He breathed, or the sunlight in which He walked. His thoughts were God's purpose for Him. This was what made Him the pattern of meekness and submission; for He was for ever bringing every thought and wish into obedience to His Father's will. This was the secret of the peace and majestic calmness which imparted such a grandeur to His demeanor in the most trying hours of life. He knew that the worst that could happen to Him was His Father's will for Him; and this was enough. He had ever at hand a retreat of perfect rest, silence, and sunshine, into which He could retire from the clamor and confusion around Him. This was the great secret He bequeathed to His followers, when He said to them at parting, "Peace I leave with you; *My* peace I give unto you." (John 10:30; 14:27)

The *Sinlessness* of Jesus has been often dwelt on as the crowning attribute of His character. The Scriptures, which so frankly record the errors of their very greatest heroes, such as Abraham and Moses, have no sins of His to record. There is no more prominent characteristic of the saints of antiquity than their penitence: the more supremely saintly they were, the more abundant and bitter were their tears and lamentations over their sinfulness. But although it is acknowledged by all that Jesus was the supreme religious figure of history, He never exhibited this characteristic of saintliness; He confessed no sin. Must it not have been because He had no sin to confess? Yet the idea of sinlessness is too negative to express the perfection of His character. He was sinless; but He was so because He was absolutely full of love. Sin against God is merely the expression of lack of love to God, and sin against man of lack of love to man. This fulness of love to His Father and His fellow-men, ruling every expression of His being, constituted the perfection of His character. (I Peter 2:22)

HIS DEITY

To the impression produced on them by their long-continued contact with their Master the Twelve owed all they became. We can not trace with any fulness at what time they began to realize the central truth of the Christianity they were afterwards to publish to the world, that behind the tenderness and majesty of this human character there was in Him something still more august, or by what stages their impressions ripened to the full conviction that in Him perfect manhood was in union with perfect Deity. This was the goal of all the revelations of Himself which He made to them. But the breakdown of their faith at His death shows how immature up till that time must have been their convictions in regard to His personality, however worthily they were able, in certain happy hours, to express their faith in Him. It was the experience of the Resurrection and Ascension which gave to the fluid impressions, which had long been accumulating in their minds, the touch by which they were made to crystallize into the immovable conviction, that in Him with whom it had been vouchsafed to them to associate so intimately, *God was manifest in the flesh.* (I Timothy 3:16)

NINE

The Year of Opposition — Its Causes

CHANGE OF SENTIMENT TOWARDS HIM

For a whole year Jesus pursued His work in Galilee with incessant energy, moving among the pitiable crowds that solicited His miraculous help, and seizing every opportunity of pouring His words of grace and truth into the ears of the multitude or of the solitary anxious inquirer. His name must have become a household word; in thousands of minds, whose depths His preaching had stirred, He must have been cherished with gratitude and love. Wider and wider rang the echoes of His fame. For a time it seemed as if all Galilee were to become His disciples.

But the twelve months had scarcely passed when it became sadly evident that this was not to be. The Galilean mind turned out to be stony ground, where the seed of the kingdom rushed quickly up, but just as quickly withered away. The change was sudden and complete, and at once altered all the features of the life of Jesus. He lingered in Galilee for six months longer; but these months were very unlike the first twelve. The voices that rose around Him were no longer the ringing shouts of gratitude and applause, but voices of opposition, bitter and blasphemous. He was no longer to be seen moving from one populous place to another in the heart of the country, welcomed everywhere by those who waited to experience or to see His miracles, and followed by thousands eager not to lose a word of His discourses. He was a fugitive, seeking the most distant and outlandish places, and accompanied only by a handful of followers. At the six months' end He left Galilee, but not, as might at one time have been anticipated, borne aloft on the wave of public acknowledgment, to make an easy conquest of the hearts of the southern part of the country, and take victorious possession of a Jerusalem unable to resist the unanimous voice of the people. (Matthew 13: 20,21)

THE CAUSES OF OPPOSITION

We must trace the causes and the progress of this change in the sentiment of the Galileans, and this sad turn in the career of Jesus.

From the very first the learned and influential classes had taken up an attitude of opposition to Him. The more worldly sections of them, indeed—the Sadducees and Herodians—for a long time paid little attention to Him. They had their own affairs to mind—their wealth, their court influence, their amusements. They cared little for a religious movement going on among the lower orders. The public rumor that one professing to be the Messiah did not excite their interest, for they did not share the popular expectations on the subject. They said to each other that this was only one more of the pretenders whom the peculiar ideas of the populace were sure to raise up from time to time. It was only when the movement seemed to them to be threatening to lead to a political revolt, which would bring down the iron hand of the Roman masters on the country, afford the Procurator an excuse for new extortions, and imperil their property and comforts, that they roused themselves to pay any attention to Him. (Matthew 24:23,24; John 11: 47,48)

Very different was it, however, with the more religious sections of the upper class—the Pharisees and scribes. They took the deepest interest in all ecclesiastical and religious phenomena. A movement of a religious kind among the populace excited their eager attention, for they themselves aimed at popular influence. A new voice with the ring of prophecy in it, or the promulgation of any new doctrine or tenet, caught their ear at once. But, above all, any one putting himself forward as the Messiah produced the utmost ferment among them; for they ardently cherished Messianic hopes, and were at the time smarting keenly under the foreign domination. In relation to the rest of the community, they corresponded to our clergy and leading religious laymen, and probably formed about the same proportion of the population, and exercised at least as great an influence as these do among us. It has been estimated that they may have numbered about six thousand. They passed for the best persons in the country, the conservators of respectability and orthodoxy. (Matthew 23:6,7)

This is perhaps the most solemn and appalling circumstance in the whole tragedy of the life of Christ, that the men who rejected, hunted down, and murdered Him, were those reputed the best in the nation, its teachers and examples, the zealous conservators of the Bible and the traditions of the past,—men who were eagerly waiting for the Messiah, who judged Jesus, as they believed, according to the Scriptures, and thought they were obeying the dictates of conscience and doing God service when they treated Him as they did. (John 16:2)

There can not fail sometimes to sweep across the mind of a reader of the Gospels a strong feeling of pity for them, and a kind of sympathy with them. Jesus was so unlike the Messiah whom they were looking for and their fathers had taught them to expect! He so completely traversed their prejudices and maxims, and dishonored so many things which they had been taught to regard as sacred! They may surely be pitied; there never was a crime like their crime, and there was never punishment like their punishment.

Yet, at bottom, what was their case? It was just this, that they were so blinded with sin that they could not discern the light. Their views of the Messiah had been distorted by centuries of worldliness and unspirituality, of which they were the like-minded heirs. They thought Jesus a sinner, because He did not conform to ordinances which they and their fathers had profanely added to those of God's Word, and because their conception of a good man, to whom He did not answer, was utterly false. Jesus supplied them with evidence enough, but He could not give them eyes to see it. Their hearts were seared, hardened, and dead. They brought their stock rules and arbitrary standards to judge Him by, and were never shaken by His greatness from the fatal attitude of criticism. He brought truth near them, but they had not the truth-loving ear to recognize the enchanting sound. He brought the whitest purity, such as archangels would have veiled their faces at, near them, but they were not overawed. He brought near them the very face of mercy and heavenly love, but their dim eyes made no response. We may indeed pity the conduct of such men as an appalling misfortune, but it is better to fear and tremble at it as appalling guilt. (Matthew 13:15; John 3:19)

One thing about Jesus which from the first excited their opposition to Him was the humbleness of His origin. He was a son of the people; He had been a carpenter; they believed He had been born in rude and wicked Galilee; He had not passed through the schools of Jeru· salem or drunk at the acknowledged wells of wisdom there. They thought that a prophet, and above all the Messiah, should have been born in Judea, reared at Jerusalem in the center of culture and religion, and allied with all that was distinguished and influential in the nation. (John 1:46; Matthew 13:55)

For the same reason they were offended with the followers He chose and the company He kept. His chosen organs were not selected from among themselves, the wise and high-born, but were uneducated laymen, poor fishermen. Nay, one of them was a publican. Nothing that Jesus did, perhaps, gave greater offence than the choice of Matthew, the tax-gatherer, to be an apostle. The tax-gatherers, as servants of the alien power, were hated by all who were patriotic and respectable, at once for their trade, their extortions, and their character. How could Jesus hope that respectable and learned men should enter a circle such as that which He had formed about Himself? Besides, He mingled freely with the lowest class of the population—with publicans, harlots, and sinners. (Matthew 9:9-12)

In Christian times we have learned to love Him for this more than anything else. We easily see that, if He really was the Savior from sin, He could not have been found in more suitable company than among those who needed salvation most. We know now how He could believe that many of the lost were more the victims of circumstance than sinners by choice, and that, if He drew the magnet across the top of the rubbish, it would attract to itself many a piece of precious metal. But no such sentiment had up till His time been born into the world. The mass of sinners outside the pale of respectability were despised and hated as the enemies of society, and no efforts were made to save them. On the contrary, all who aimed at religious distinction avoided their very touch as a defilement. Simon the Pharisee, when he was entertaining Jesus, never doubted that, if He had been a prophet and known who the woman was who was touching Him, He would have driven her off. Such was the sentiment of the time. (Luke 7:36-50)

Yet when Jesus brought into the world the new sentiment, and showed them the divine face of mercy, they ought to have recognized it. If their hearts had not been utterly hard and cruel, they would have leapt up to welcome this revelation of a diviner humanity. The sight of sinners forsaking their evil ways, of wicked women sobbing for their lost lives, and extortioners like Zaccheus becoming earnest and generous, ought to have delighted them. But it did not, and they only hated Jesus for His

compassion, calling Him a friend of publicans and sinners. (Luke 7:36-50; 19:1-10)

*A third and very serious ground of their opposition
was, that He did not Himself practice, nor encourage His
disciples to practice, many ritual observances,* such as
fasts, punctilious washing of the hands before meals, and
so forth, which were then considered the marks of a
saintly man. It has been already explained how these
practices arose. The original intention was good, but the
result was deplorable. It was soon forgotten that they
were merely human inventions; they were supposed to be
binding by divine action; and they were multiplied, till
they regulated every hour of the day and every action of
life. They were made the substitutes for real piety and
morality by the majority; and to tender consciences they
were an intolerable burden. But no one doubted their
authority, and the careful observance of them was reputed the badge of a godly life. Jesus regarded them as
the great evil of the time. But the result was, that He
was looked upon as both an ungodly man Himself, and a
deceiver of the people. (Mark 7:1-13; Matthew 9:14-15)

It was especially in regard to the Sabbath that this
difference between Him and the religious teachers came
out. In this field their inventions of restrictions and arbitrary rules had run into the most portentous extrava-
gance, till they had changed the day of rest, joy, and
blessing into an intolerable burden. He was in the habit
of performing His cures on the Sabbath. They thought
such work a breach of the command. He exposed the
wrongness of their objections again and again, by ex-
plaining the nature of the institution itself as "made for
man," by reference to the practice of ancient saints, and

even by the analogy of some of their own practices on the holy day. But they were not convinced; and, as He continued His practice in spite of their objections, this remained a standing and bitter ground of their hatred. (Luke 13:11-17; Mark 2:27; John 5:15-18)

It will be easily understood that, having arrived at these conclusions on such low grounds, they were utterly disinclined to listen to Him when He put forward His higher claims—when He announced Himself as the Messiah, professed to forgive sins, and threw out intimations of His high relation to God. Having concluded that He was an imposter and deceiver, they regarded such assertions as hideous blasphemies, and could not help wishing to stop the mouth which uttered them.

It "may cause surprise," that they were not convinced by His miracles. If He really performed the numerous and stupendous miracles which are recorded of Him, how could they resist such evidence of His divine mission? The debate held with the authorities by the tough reasoner whom Jesus cured of blindness, and whose case is recorded in the ninth chapter of John, shows how sorely they may sometimes have been pressed with such reasoning. But they had satisfied themselves with an audacious reply to it. They had come to the conclusion that He had not been sent from God; and so they attributed His miracles to an alliance with the powers of darkness. Jesus met this blasphemous construction with the utmost force of holy indignation and conclusive argument; but it is easy to see that it was a position in which minds like those of His opponents might entrench themselves with the sense of much security. (Matthew 9:34; 12:22-30; John 12:37)

Very early they had formed their adverse judgment of Him, and they never changed it. Even during His first year in Judea they had pretty well decided against Him. When the news of His success in Galilee spread, it filled them with consternation, and they sent deputations from Jerusalem to act in concert with their local adherents in opposing Him. Even during His year of joy He clashed with them again and again. At first He treated them with consideration and appealed to their reason and heart. But He soon saw that this was hopeless and accepted their opposition as inevitable. He exposed the hollowness of their pretensions to His audiences and warned His disciples against them. Meanwhile they did everything to poison the public mind against Him. They succeeded only too well. When, at the year's end, the tide of His popularity began to recede, they pressed their advantage, assailing Him more and more boldly. (Matthew 23:14,24)

They even succeeded thus early in arousing the cold minds of the Sadducees and Herodians against Him, no doubt by persuading them that He was fomenting a popular revolt, which would endanger the throne of their master Herod, who reigned over Galilee. That mean and characterless prince himself also became His presecutor. About this very time he had murdered John the Baptist. It was one of the meanest and foulest crimes recorded in history, an awful instance of the way in which sin leads to sin, and of the malicious perseverance with which a wicked woman will compass her revenge. Soon after it was committed, his courtiers came to tell him of the supposed political designs of Jesus. But when he heard of the new prophet, an awful thought stirred through his guilty conscience. "It is John the Baptist," he cried,

"There is a lad here with five barley loaves and two fish."

"whom I beheaded, he is risen from the dead." Yet he desired to see Him, his curiosity getting the better of his terror. It was the desire of the lion to see the lamb. Jesus never responded to his invitation. Jesus had to keep out of his way, and no doubt this helped along with more important things to change the character of His life in Galilee during the last six months of His stay there. (Matthew 14:1-13; Mark 6:14-16)

At last, however, the decisive hour seemed to have arrived. It was just at that great turning-point to which allusion has frequently been made—the end of the twelve months in Galilee. Jesus had heard of the Baptist's death, and immediately hurried away into a desert place with His disciples, to brood and talk over the tragic event. He sailed to the eastern side of the lake, and, landing on the grassy plain of Bethsaida, went up to a hill with the Twelve. But soon at its feet there gathered an immense multitude to hear and see Him.

Ever ready to sacrifice Himself for others, He descended to address and heal them. The evening came on, as His discourse prolonged itself, when, moved with a great access of compassion for the helpless multitude, He wrought the stupendous miracle of feeding the five thousand. Its effect was overwhelming. They became instantaneously convinced that This was none other than the Messiah, and, having only one conception of what this meant, they endeavored to take Him by force and make Him a king; that is, to force Him to become the leader of a Messianic revolt, by which they might wrest the throne from Cæsar and the princelings he had set up over the different provinces. (Mark 6:17-44; John 6:15)

It seemed the crowning hour of success. But to Jesus Himself it was an hour of sad and bitter shame. This was all that His year's work had come to! This was the conception they yet had of Him! And they were to determine the course of His future action, instead of humbly asking what He would have them to do! He accepted it as the decisive indication of the effect of His work in Galilee. He saw how shallow were its results. He fled from their carnal desires, and the very next day, meeting them again at Capernaum, He told them how much they had been mistaken in Him; they were looking for a Bread-king, who would give them idleness and plenty, mountains of loaves, rivers of milk, every comfort without labor. What He had to give was the bread of eternal life. (John 6:26,47-51)

His discourse was like a stream of cold water directed upon the fiery enthusiasm of the crowd. From that hour His cause in Galilee was doomed; "many of His disciples went back and walked no more with Him." It was what He intended. It was Himself who struck the fatal blow at His popularity. He resolved to devote Himself thenceforward to the few who really understood Him and were capable of being the adherents of a spiritual enterprise. (John 6:66)

TEN

The Year of Opposition —
The Changed Aspect of His Ministry

THE SIFTING OF THE DISCIPLES

Yet, although the people of Galilee at large had shown themselves unworthy of Him, there was a considerable remnant that proved true. At the center of it were the apostles; but there were also others, probably several hundreds. These now became the objects of His special care. He had saved them as brands plucked from the burning, when Galilee as a whole deserted Him. For them it must have been a time of crucial trial. Their views were to a large extent those of the populace. They also expected a Messiah of worldly splendor. They had indeed learned to include deeper and more spiritual elements in their conception, but, along with these, it still contained the traditional and material ones. It must have been a painful mystery to them that Jesus should so long delay the assumption of the crown.

The Baptist's death must have been an awful shock to them. If Jesus was the Mighty One they thought Him, how could He allow His friend to come to such an end?

Still they held on to Him. They showed what it was which kept them by their answer to Him, when, after the dispersion which followed the discourse at Capernaum, He put to them the sad question, "Will ye also go away?" They replied, "Lord, to whom shall we go? Thou hast the words of eternal life." Their opinions were not clear; they were in a mist of perplexities; but they knew that from Him they were getting eternal life. This held them close to Him, and made them willing to wait till He should make things clear. (John 6:68)

During the last six months He spent in Galilee, He abandoned to a large extent His old work of preaching and miracle-working, and devoted Himself to the instruction of these adherents. He made long circuits with them in the most distant parts of the province, avoiding publicity as much as possible. Thus we find Him at Tyre and Sidon, far to the northwest; at Cæsarea-Philippi, on the far northeast; and in Decapolis, to the south and east of the lake. (Matthew 15:21; Mark 7:31)

These journeys, or rather flights, were due partly to the bitter opposition of the Pharisees, partly to fear of Herod, but chiefly to the desire to be alone with His disciples. The precious result of them was seen in an incident which happened at Cæsarea-Philippi. Jesus began to ask His disciples what were the popular views about Himself, and they told Him the various conjectures which were flying about,—that He was a prophet, that He was Elias, that He was John the Baptist, and so on. "But whom say ye that I am? He asked; and Peter answered for them all, "Thou art the Christ, the Son of the living God." This was the deliberate and decisive conviction by which they were determined to abide, whatever might come. Jesus received the confession with great joy, and at once recognized in those who had made it the nucleus of the future church, which was to be built on the truth to which they had given expression. (Matthew 16:13-19)

But this attainment only prepared them for a new trial of faith. From that time, we are told, He began to inform them of His approaching sufferings and death. These now stood out clearly before His own mind as the only issue of His career to be looked for. He had hinted as much to them before, but, with that delicate and loving consideration which always graduated His teaching to their capacity, He did not refer to it often. (Matthew 16:21)

But now they were in some degree able to bear it; and, as it was inevitable and near at hand, He kept insisting on it constantly. But they themselves tell us they did not in the least understand Him. In common with all their countrymen, they expected a Messiah who should sit on the throne of David, and of whose reign there should be no end. It was to them utterly incomprehensible that, instead of reigning, He should be killed on His arrival in Jerusalem. They thought He was only using one of the parabolic sayings of which He was so fond, His real meaning being that the present lowly form of His work was to die and disappear, and His cause rise, as it were, out of the grave in a glorious and triumphant shape. He endeavored to undeceive them, going more and more minutely into the details of His approaching sufferings. But their minds could not take the truth in. How completely even the best of them failed to do so is shown by the frequent wranglings among them at this period as to which of them should in the approaching kingdom be the greatest, and by the request of Salome for her sons, that they should sit the one on the right and the other on the left hand in His kingdom. When they left Galilee and went up towards Jerusalem, it was with the conviction that "the kingdom of God should immediately appear," —that is, that Jesus, on arriving in the capital, would throw off the guise of humiliation He had hitherto worn, and, overcoming all opposition by some forthputting of His concealed glory, take His place on the throne of His fathers. (Luke 9:44,45; 19:11; Matthew 20:28,29)

HIS OWN THOUGHTS AT THIS PERIOD

What were the thoughts and feelings of Jesus Himself during this year? To Him also it was a year of sore trial. During the twelve months of successful work in Galilee, He was borne up with the joy of sustained achievement. But now He became, in the truest sense, the Man of Sorrows. Behind Him was His rejection by Galilee. The sorrow which He felt is to be measured only by the greatness of His love to the souls He sought to save, and the depth of His devotion to His work. In front of Him was His rejection at Jerusalem. That was now certain; it rose up and stood out constantly and unmistakably, meeting His eyes as often as He turned them to the future. It absorbed His thoughts. (Isaiah 53:3-6)

He was very much in prayer. This had all along been His delight and resource. In His busiest period, when He was often so tired with the labors of the day that at the approach of evening He was ready to fling Himself down in utter fatigue, He would nevertheless escape away from the crowds and His disciples to the mountain-top, and spend the whole night in lonely communion with His

Father. But now He was far oftener alone than ever before, setting forth His case to His God. (Luke 9:18)

His prayers received a splendid answer in the Transfiguration. That glorious scene took place in the middle of the year of opposition, just before He quitted Galilee and set forth on the journey of doom. It was intended partly for the sake of the three disciples who accompanied Him to the mountain-top, to strengthen their faith and make them fit to strengthen their brethren. But it was chiefly intended for Himself. It was a great gift of His Father, an acknowledgment of His faithfulness up to this point, and a preparation for what lay before Him. It was about the decease He was to accomplish at Jerusalem He conversed with His great predecessors, Moses and Elias, who could thoroughly sympathize with Him, and whose work His death was to fulfill. (Luke 9:28-36)

Immediately after this event He left Galilee and went south. He spent six months on His way to Jerusalem. It was part of His mission to preach the kingdom over the whole land, and He did so. He sent seventy of His disciples on before Him to prepare the villages and towns to receive Him. Again in this new field the same manifestations as Galilee had witnessed during the first months of His labors there showed themselves,—the multitudes following Him, the wonderful cures, and so forth. (Luke 10:1)

We have not records of this period sufficient to enable us to follow Him step by step. We find Him on the borders of Samaria, in Peræa, on the banks of the Jordan, in Bethany, in the village of Ephraim. But Jerusalem was His goal. His face was set like a flint for it. Sometimes He was so absorbed in the anticipation of what was to befall Him there, that His disciples, following His swift, mute figure along the highway, were amazed and afraid. Now and then, indeed, He would relax a little, as when He was blessing the little children or visiting the home of His friends at Bethany. But His mood at this period was more stern, absorbed, and highly strung than ever before. Everything denoted that the end was drawing near. He was in the grip of His grand purpose of atoning for the sins of the world, and His soul was straitened till it should be accomplished. (Matthew 19:13-15; Luke 10:38-42)

THE SANHEDRIN RESOLVES ON HIS DEATH

The catastrophe drew nigh apace. He paid two brief visits to Jerusalem, before the final one, during His last six months. On both occasions the opposition of the authorities assumed the most menacing form. They endeavored to arrest Him on the first occasion, and took up stones to stone Him on the second. They had already issued a decree that any one acknowledging Him to be the Messiah should be excommunicated. But it was the excitement produced in the popular mind by the raising of Lazarus at the very gates of the ecclesiastical citadel which finally convinced the authorities that they could not satisfy themselves with anything short of His death. So they resolved in council. This took place only a month or two before the end came, and it drove Him for the time from the neighborhood of Jerusalem. But He retired only until the hour which His Father had appointed Him should strike. (John 11:45-54)

ELEVEN

The Approaching End

THE PASSOVER

At length the third year of His ministry verged towards its close, and the revolving seasons brought round the great annual feast of the Passover. It is said that as many as two or three millions of strangers were gathered in Jerusalem on such an occasion. They not only flocked from every part of Palestine, but came over sea and land from all the countries in which the seed of Abraham were dispersed, in order to celebrate the event in which their national history began. They were brought together by very various motives. Some came with the solemn thoughts and deep religious joy of minds responsive to the memories of the venerable occasion. Some looked forward chiefly to reunion with relatives and friends who had been long parted from them by residence in distant places. (Luke 22:7)

But this year the minds of tens of thousands were full of an unusual excitement, and they came up to the capital expecting to see something more remarkable than they had ever witnessed there before. They hoped to see Jesus at the feast, and entertained many vague forebodings as to what might happen in connection with Him. His name was the word oftenest passing from mouth to mouth among the pilgrim bands that crowded along the highways. Nearly all His own disciples no doubt were there, and were ardently cherishing the hope that at last in this concourse of the nation He would throw off the guise of humility which concealed His glory, and in some irresistible way demonstrate His Messiahship. The authorities in Jerusalem, too, awaited His coming with very mingled feelings. They hoped that some turn of events might give them the chance of at last suppressing Him; but they could not help fearing that He might appear at the head of a provincial following which would place them at His mercy.

THE FINAL BREACH WITH THE NATION

Six days before the Passover began, He arrived in Bethany, the village of His friends Martha, Mary, and Lazarus, which lay half-an-hour from the city on the other side of the summit of the Mount of Olives. It was a convenient place to lodge during the feast, and He took up His quarters with His friends. The solemnities were to begin on a Thursday, so that it was on the previous Friday He arrived there. He had been accompanied the last twenty miles of His journey by an immense multitude of the pilgrims, to whom He was the center of interest. They had seen Him healing blind Bartimæus at Jericho, and the miracle had produced among them extraordinary excitement. When they reached Bethany, the village was ringing with the recent resurrection of Lazarus, and they carried on the news to the crowds who had already arrived from all quarters in Jerusalem, that Jesus had come. (John 12:1; Mark 10:46-52)

Accordingly, when, after resting over the Sabbath in Bethany, He came forth on the Sunday morning to proceed to the city, He found the streets of the village and the neighboring roads thronged with a vast crowd, consisting partly of those who had accompanied Him on the Friday, partly of other companies who had come up behind Him from Jericho and heard of the miracles as they came along, and partly of those who, having heard that He was at hand, had flocked out from Jerusalem to see Him. They welcomed Him with enthusiasm, and began to shout "Hosanna to the Son of David! Blessed is He that cometh in the name of the Lord! Hosanna in the highest!" It was a Messianic demonstration such as He had formerly avoided. (Matthew 21:9)

The hour had come when no considerations could permit Him any longer to conceal from the nation the character in which He presented Himself and the claim He made on its faith. But, in yielding to the desires of the multitude that He should assume the style of a king, He made it unmistakable in what sense He accepted the honor. He sent for an ass-colt, and, His disciples having spread their garments on it, rode at the head of the crowd. Not armed to the teeth or bestriding a war-horse did He come, but as the King of simplicity and peace. The procession swept over the brow of Olivet and down the mountain-side; it crossed the Kedron, and, mounting the slope which led to the gate of the city, passed on through the streets to the temple. It swelled as it went, great numbers hurrying from every quarter to join it; the shouts rang louder and more loud; the processionists

broke off twigs from the palms and olives, as they passed, and waved them in triumph. The citizens of Jerusalem ran to their doors and bent over their balconies to
look, and asked, "Who is this?" to which the processionists replied with provincial pride, "This is Jesus, the
prophet of Nazareth." It was, in fact, an entirely provincial demonstration. The authorities knew only too
well what it meant, and beheld it with rage and dread.
They came to Jesus, and ordered Him to bid His followers hold their peace, hinting no doubt that, if He did not
do so, the Roman garrison, which was stationed in the
immediate vicinity, would pounce on Him and them, and
punish the city for an act of treason to Cæsar. (Luke
19:28-44; John 12:12-19)

Jesus had formally made offer of Himself to the capital and the authorities of the nation, but met with no response. The provincial recognition of His claims was
insufficient to carry a national assent. He accepted the
decision as final. The multitude expected a signal from
Him, and in their excited mood would have obeyed it,
whatever it might have been. But He gave them none,
and, after looking round about Him for a little in the
temple, left them and returned to Bethany. Doubtless
the disappointment of the multitude was extreme. (John
1:11; Matthew 21:17)

On Monday and Tuesday He appeared again in the city
and engaged in His old work of healing and teaching.
But on the second of these days the authorities inter-
posed. Pharisees, Sadducees, and Herodians, high priests,
priests, and scribes were for once combined in a common
cause. They came to Him, as He taught in the temple,
and demanded by what authority He did such things. In

all the pomp of official costume, of social pride and popular renown, they set themselves against the simple Galilean, while the multitudes looked on. They entered into a keen and prolonged controversy with Him on points selected beforehand, putting forward their champions of debate to entangle Him in His talk, their distinct object being, either to discredit Him with the audience or to elicit something from His lips in the heat of argument which might form a ground of accusation against Him before the civil authority. (Matthew 21:18, 23-27)

Thus, for example, they asked Him if it was lawful to give tribute to Cæsar. If He answered *Yes*, they knew that His popularity would perish on the instant, for it would be a complete contradiction of the popular Messianic ideas. If, on the contrary, He answered *No*, they would accuse Him of treason before the Roman governor. But Jesus was far more than a match for them. Hour by hour He steadfastly met the attack. His straightforwardness put their duplicity to shame. He convicted them of such ignorance or lack of candor as completely put them to shame before the onlookers. Then, when He had silenced them, He let loose the storm of His indignation, and delivered against them the philippic which is recorded in the twenty-third chapter of Matthew. He exposed their hypocritical practices in sentences that fell like strokes of lightning and made them a scorn and laughing-stock, not only to the hearers then, but to all the world since. (Matthew 22:15-46; 23)

It was the final breach between Him and them. They had been utterly humiliated before the whole people, over whom they were set in authority and honor. They felt it to be intolerable, and resolved not to lose an hour in seeking their revenge. That very evening the Sanhedrin met in passionate mood to devise a plan for making away with Him. But circumstances checked their cruel haste. At least the forms of justice would have to be gone through; and besides, Jesus evidently enjoyed an immense popularity among the strangers who filled the city. What might not the idle crowd do if He were arrested before their eyes? It was necessary to wait till the mass of the pilgrims had left the city. They had just, with great reluctance, arrived at this conclusion, when they received a most unexpected and gratifying surprise. One of His own disciples appeared, and offered to betray Him for a price. (Luke 22:1-6)

Judas Iscariot is the byword of the human race. It is inconceivable that Jesus would have made him an apostle if there had not at one time been some noble enthusiasm in him, and some attachment to Himself. That he was a man of superior energy and administrative ability may be inferred from the fact that he was made the purse-bearer of the apostolic company. But there was a canker at the root of his character, which gradually absorbed all that was excellent in him, and became a tyrannical passion. It was the love of money. Judas' earthly views became more and more engrossing. The purity and unworldliness of Jesus irritated him; why did He not bring on the kingdom at once, and then preach as much as He chose afterwards? At last he began to suspect that there was to be no kingdom such as he had hoped for. He felt that he had been deceived, and began not only to despise but even hate his Master. He saw that the ship was sinking and resolved to get out of it. He carried out his resolution in such a way as both to gratify his master-passion and secure the favor of the authorities. His offer came to them just at the right moment. They closed with it greedily, and, having arranged the price with the miserable man, sent him away to find a convenient opportunity for the betrayal. He found it sooner than they expected—on the next night after the dastardly bargain had been concluded. (Matthew 26:14-16)

JESUS IN THE PROSPECT OF DEATH

Unspeakably great as He always was, it may be reverently said that He was never so great as during those days of direst calamity. He came to Jerusalem well aware that He was about to die. For a whole year the fact had been staring Him constantly in the face, and the long-looked-for had come at last. It was not, however, without good reason. It is an instinct perfectly innocent. of the most diverse emotions—anguish and ecstasy, the most prolonged and crushing depression, the most triumphant joy and the most majestic peace—swayed hither and thither within Him like the moods of a vast ocean.

Some have hesitated to attribute to Him aught of that shrinking from death which is natural to man; but surely without good reason. It is an instinct perfectly innocent. Remember how young He was—only three-and-thirty; the currents of life were powerful in Him. To have these strong currents rolled back and the light and warmth of life quenched in the cold waters of death must have been utterly repugnant to Him.

An incident which happened on the Monday caused Him a great shock of this instinctive pain. Some Greeks who had come to the feast expressed through two of the apostles their desire for an interview with Him. There were many heathens in different parts of the Greek-speaking world who at this period had found refuge from the atheism and disgusting immorality of the times in the religion of the Jews. Only two or three times in the course of His ministry does He seem to have been brought into contact with representatives of the world lying outside the limits of His own people, His mission being exclusively to the lost sheep of the house of Israel. But on every such occasion He met with a faith, a courtesy and nobility, which He Himself contrasted with the unbelief, rudeness, and pettiness of the Jews. Instead of responding to their request, He became abstracted, His face darkened, and His frame was shaken with the tremor of an inward conflict. But He soon recovered Himself, and gave expression to the thoughts on which in those days He was steadying up His soul: "Except a corn of wheat fall into the ground and die, it abideth alone; but if it die, it bringeth forth much fruit." "And I, if I be lifted up from the earth, will draw all men unto Me." Death was what His Father had appointed for Him. This was the last and deepest consolation with which He soothed His humble and trustful soul on this as on every similar occasion: "Now is my soul troubled; and what shall I say? Father, save me from this hour: but for this cause came I unto this hour. Father, glorify Thyself." (John 12:20-36)

Death approached Him with every terrible accompaniment. He was to fall a victim to the treachery of a follower of His own, whom He had chosen and loved. His life was to be taken by the hands of His own nation, in the city of His heart. He had come to exalt His nation to heaven, and had loved her with a devotion. But His death would bring down the blight of a thousand curses on Palestine and Jerusalem. How clearly He foresaw what was coming was shown by the memorable prophetic discourse of the twenty-fourth of Matthew, which He spoke on Tuesday afternoon to His disciples, sitting on the side of Mount Olivet, with the doomed city at His feet. He who would have taken her to His heart, as the hen gathers her chickens under her wings, saw the eagles already in the air, flying fast to rend her in pieces. (Matthew 23:37)

In the evenings of this week He went out to Bethany; but in all probability He spent most of the nights alone in the open air. He wandered about in the solitude of the hill-top and among the olive-groves and gardens with which the sides of the mount were covered. Yet He was not alone. His Father was with Him. He hushed His spirit with the sense that His Father's perfect love and wisdom were appointing all that was happening to Him, and that He was glorifying His Father and fulfilling the work given Him to do. This could banish every fear, and fill Him with a joy unspeakable and full of glory. (Luke 21:37; John 12:27; 13:1)

At last the end drew very near. The Thursday evening arrived, when in every house in Jerusalem the Passover was eaten. Jesus also with the Twelve sat down to eat it. He knew that it was His last night before death. Happily there has been preserved to us a full account of it, with which every Christian mind is familiar. His soul overflowed in indescribable tenderness and grandeur. Some shadows indeed fell across His spirit in the earlier hours of the evening. But they soon passed; and throughout the scenes of the washing of the disciples' feet, the eating of the Passover, the institution of the Lord's Supper, the farewell address, and the great high-priestly prayer, the whole glory of His character shone out. He completely resigned Himself to the genial impulses of friendship, His love to His own flowing forth without limit; and, as if He had forgotten all their imperfections, He rejoiced in the anticipation of their future successes and the triumph of His cause. He looked on His own work just about to be completed. It was as if the Passion were already past, and the glory of His Exaltation were already breaking around Him.

But the reaction came very soon. Rising from the table at midnight, they passed through the streets and out of the town by the eastern gate of the city, and, crossing the Kedron, reached a well-known haunt of His at the foot of Olivet, the garden of Gethsemane. Here ensued the awful and memorable Agony. But we fear to analyze the elements of the scene. We know that any conception of ours must be utterly unable to exhaust its meaning. How, above all, can we estimate in the faintest degree the chief element in it,—the crushing, scorching pressure of the sin of the world, which He was then expiating? But the struggle ended in a complete victory. While the poor disciples were sleeping away the hours of preparation for the crisis which was at hand, He had thoroughly equipped Himself for it; He had fought down the last remnants of temptation; the bitterness of death was past; and He was able to go through the scenes which followed with a calmness which nothing could ruffle, and a majesty which converted His trial and crucifixion into the pride and glory of humanity. (Mark 14:32-42; Luke 22:39-46)

At the cross they observed it all.

TWELVE

The Trial

HIS ARREST

Through the branches of the olives He saw, moving in the moonlight down the opposite slope, the mass of His enemies coming to arrest Him. The traitor was at their head. He was well acquainted with his Master's haunt and probably hoped to find Him there asleep. For this reason he had chosen the midnight hour for his dark deed. It suited his employers well too, for they were afraid to lay hands on Jesus in the day-time. But they knew how it would overawe His friends, if, getting His trial over during the night, they could show Him in the morning, when the populace awoke, already a condemned criminal in the hands of the executors of the law. (Matthew 26:47-50)

They had brought lanterns and torches with them, thinking they might find their victim crouching in some cave, or that they might have to pursue Him through the wood. But He came forth to meet them at the entrance to the garden, and they quailed like cravens before His majestic looks and withering words. He freely surrendered Himself into their hands, and they led Him back to the city. It was probably about midnight; and the remaining hours of the night and the early hours of the morning were occupied with the legal proceedings which had to be gone through, before they could gratify their thirst for His life. (John 18:1-11)

REASONS FOR DOUBLE TRIAL

There were two trials, an ecclesiastical one and a civil one, in each of which there were three stages. The former took place, first before Annas, then before Caiaphas and an informal committee of the Sanhedrin, and, lastly, before a regular meeting of this court; the latter took place, first before Pilate, then before Herod, and, lastly, before Pilate again.

The reason for this double legal process was the political situation of the country. Judea, as has been already explained, was directly subject to the Roman empire, forming a part of the province of Syria, and being governed by a Roman officer, who resided at Cæsarea. But it was not the practice of Rome to strip those countries which she had subdued of all the forms of native government. Though she ruled with an iron hand, yet she conceded to the conquered as many of the insignia as possible of their ancient power. She was especially tolerant in matters of religion. Thus the Sanhedrin, the supreme ecclesiastical court of the Jews, was still permitted to try all religious causes. Only, if the sentence passed was a capital one, its execution could not take place without the case being tried over again before the governor. The crime of which Jesus was accused was one which naturally came before the ecclesiastical court. This court passed on Him a death sentence. But it had not the power to carry it out. It had to hand Him on to the tribunal of the governor, who happened at the time to be in the capital, which he generally visited at the Passover.

ECCLESIASTCAL TRIAL

. Jesus was conducted first to the palace of Annas. He was an old man of seventy, who had been high priest a score of years before, and still retained the title, though his son-in-law Caiaphas was the actual high-priest. His age, ability, and family influence gave him immense social weight, and he was the virtual, though not formal, head of the Sanhedrin. He did not try Jesus, but merely wished to see Him and ask a few questions; so that He was very soon led away from the palace of Annas to that of Caiaphas, which probably formed part of the same group of official buildings. (John 18:12-14, 19-23)

Caiaphas, as ruling high-priest, was president of the Sanhedrin, before which Jesus was tried. A legal meeting of this court could not be held before sunrise, perhaps about six o'clock. But there were many of its members already on the spot, who had been drawn together by their interest in the case. They were eager to get to work, both to gratify their own dislike to Him and to prevent the interference of the populace with their proceedings. Accordingly, they resolved to hold an informal meeting at once, at which the accusation, evidence and so forth might be put into shape, so that, when the legal hour for opening their doors arrived, there might be nothing to do but to repeat the necessary formalities and carry Him off to the governor. This was done; and, while Jerusalem slept, these eager judges hurried forward their dark designs. (Matthew 26:57-68; Mark 14:53-65; Luke 22:54,63-65)

The high-priest began with questioning Him as to His disciples and doctrine, evidently with the view of discovering whether He had taught any revolutionary tenets, which might form a ground of accusation before the governor. But Jesus repelled the insinuation, indignantly asserting that He had ever spoken openly before the world and demanded a statement and proof of any evil He had done. This unusual reply induced one of the minions of the court to smite Him on the mouth with His fist—an act which the court apparently did not rebuke, and which showed what amount of justice He had to expect at the hands of His judges. (John 18:19-23)

An attempt was then made to bring proof against Him, a number of witnesses repeating various statements they had heard Him make, out of which it was hoped an accusation might be constructed. But it turned out a total failure. The witnesses could not agree among themselves; and when at last two were got to unite in a distorted report of a saying of His early ministry, which appeared to have some color of criminality, it turned out to be a thing so paltry that it would have been absurd to appear with it before the governor as the ground of a serious charge. (Mark 14:56)

They were resolved on His death, but the prey seemed slipping out of their hands. Jesus looked on in absolute silence, while contradictory testimonies of the witnesses demolished each other. He quietly took His natural position far above His judges. They felt it; and at last the president, in a transport of rage and irritation, started up and commanded Him to speak. The humiliating spectacle going on in the witness box and the silent dignity of Jesus were beginning to trouble even these consciences assembled in the dead of night. (Luke 22:67,68)

The case had completely broken down, when Caiaphas rose from his seat, and, with theatrical solemnity, asked the question: "I adjure Thee by the living God, that Thou tell us whether Thou be the Christ the Son of God." It was a question asked merely in order to induce Jesus to criminate Himself. Yet He who had kept silence when He might have spoken now spoke when He might have been silent. With great solemnity He answered in the affirmative, that He was the Messiah and the Son of God. Nothing more was needed by His judges. They unanimously pronounced Him guilty of blasphemy and worthy of death. (Mark 14:55-64; Matthew 26:57-66)

The whole trial had been conducted with precipitancy and total disregard of the formalities proper to a court of law. Everything was dictated by the desire to arrive at guilt, not justice. The same persons were both prosecutors and judges. No witnesses for the defence were thought of.

The trial was now looked upon as past, the legal proceedings after sunrise being a mere formality, which would be got over in a few minutes. Accordingly, Jesus was given up as a condemned man to the cruelty of the jailors and the mob. Then ensued a scene over which one would gladly draw a veil. There broke forth on Him a brutality of abuse which makes the blood run cold. They smote Him with their fists, they spat on Him, they blindfolded Him, and, in derision of His prophetic claims, bade

Him prophesy who struck Him, as they took their turn of smiting Him. But we will not dwell on a scene so disgraceful to human nature. (Mark 14:65)

CIVIL TRIAL

It was probably between six and seven in the morning when they conducted Jesus, bound with chains, to the residence of the governor. What a spectacle that was! The priests, teachers, and judges of the Jewish nation leading their Messiah to ask the Gentile to put Him to death! This was all that had come of God's causing His glory for so many centuries to pass before their eyes! Yet God was not mocked. His designs march down through history with resistless tread, waiting not on the will of man; and even this tragic hour was destined to demonstrate the depths of His wisdom and love. (Mark 15:1)

The man before whose judgment-seat Jesus was about to appear was Pontius Pilate, who had been governor of Judea for six years. He was a typical Roman, not of the antique, simple stamp, but of the imperial period; a man not without some remains of the ancient Roman justice in his soul; yet pleasure-loving, imperious, and corrupt. He hated the Jews whom he ruled, and, in times of irritation, freely shed their blood. They returned his hatred with cordiality, and accused him of every crime, maladministration, cruelty, and robbery. He visited Jerusalem as seldom as possible. When he did visit it, he stayed in the magnificent palace of Herod the Great; it being common for the officers sent by Rome into conquered countries to occupy the palaces of the displaced sovereigns.

Up the broad avenue, which led through a fine park, laid out with walks, ponds, and trees of various kinds, to the front of the building, the Sanhedrists and the crowd which had joined the procession, as it moved on through the streets, conducted Jesus. The court was held in the open air, on a mosaic pavement in front of that portion of the palace which united its two colossal wings.

The Jewish authorities had hoped that Pilate would accept their decision as his own, and without going into the merits of the case, pass the sentence they desired. This was frequently done by provincial governors, especially in matters of religion, which, as foreigners, they could not be expected to understand. Accordingly, when he asked what the crime of Jesus was, they replied, "If He were not a malefactor, we would not have delivered Him up unto thee." But he was not in the mood of concession, and told them that, if he was not to try the culprit, they must be content with such a punishment as their law permitted them to inflict. (John 18:28-31)

Forced against their hopes to bring forward formal charges, the Jewish authorities poured out a volley of accusations, out of which these three clearly emerged,— that (1) He had perverted the nation, that (2) He forbade to pay the Roman tribute, and that (3) He set Himself up as a king. In the Sanhedrin they had condemned Him for blasphemy; but such a charge would have been improper before Pilate. They had therefore to invent new charges, which might represent Jesus as formidable to the government. In doing so, they resorted not only to gross hypocrisy, but even to deliberate falsehood. (Luke 23:1-3)

Pilate understood their pretended zeal for the Roman authority. Rising from his seat to escape the fanatical cries of the mob, he took Jesus inside the palace to ex-

amine Him. It was a solemn moment for himself, though
he knew it not. What a terrible fate it was which brought
him to the spot at this time! He had no idea of the issues
he was deciding. It could not occur to him that, though
he appeared to be the judge, yet both he and the system
he represented were on trial before One whose perfection
judged and exposed every man and every system which
approached Him. He questioned Him in regard to the
accusations brought against Him, asking especially if He
pretended to be a king. Jesus replied that He made no
such claim in the political sense, but only in a spiritual
sense, as King of the Truth. Pilate was convinced that,
as he had supposed, there lurked nothing of the dema-
gogue or Messianic revolutionist behind this pure, peace-
ful, and melancholy face; and, returning to the tribunal,
he announced to His accusers that he had acquitted Him.
(Luke 23:3,4; John 18:33-38)

The announcement was received with shrieks of disappointed rage and the loud reiteration of the charges
against Him. It was a thoroughly Jewish spectacle.
Many a time had this fanatical mob overcome the wishes
and decisions of their foreign masters by the sheer force
of clamor and pertinacity. But he was a true son of the
system in which he had been brought up—the statecraft
of compromise and maneuver. Amidst the cries with
which they assailed his ears he was glad to hear one
which offered him an excuse for getting rid of the whole
business. They were shouting that Jesus had excited the
populace "throughout all Jewry, beginning from Galilee
unto this place." It occurred to him that Herod, the ruler
of Galilee, was in town, and that he might get rid of the
troublesome affair by handing it over to him; for it was
a common procedure in Roman law to transfer a culprit

from the tribunal of the territory in which he was arrested to that of the territory in which he was domiciled. Accordingly, he sent Him away in the hands of his bodyguard, and accompanied by His indefatigable accusers, to the palace of Herod. (Luke 23:5-7)

They found this princeling, who had come to Jerusalem to attend the feast, delighted to see Jesus, whose fame had so long been ringing through the territory over which he ruled. He came up to the Passover merely for the sake of the excitement. The appearance of Jesus seemed to promise a new sensation, of which he and his court were often sorely in want; for he hoped to see Him work a miracle. He was a man utterly incapable of taking a serious view of anything, and even overlooked the business about which the Jews were so eager, for he began to pour out a flood of rambling questions and remarks, without pausing for any reply. At last, however, he exhausted himself, and waited for the response of Jesus. But he waited in vain, for Jesus did not vouchsafe him one word of any kind. But Herod was utterly incapable of feeling the annihilating force of such silent disdain. He and his men of war set Jesus at naught, and sent Him back to Pilate. In this guise He retraced His weary steps to the tribunal of the Roman. (Luke 23:8-11)

Then ensued a course of procedure on the part of Pilate by which he made himself an image of the time-server, to be exhibited to the centuries. It was evidently his duty, when Jesus returned from Herod, to pronounce at once the sentence of acquittal. But, instead of doing so, he resorted to expediency, and proposed to the Jews that, as both he and Herod had found Him innocent, he should scourge and then release Him; the scourging being a sop to their rage, and the release a tribute to justice. (Luke 23:13-16)

The carrying out of this monstrous proposal was, however, interrupted by an incident which seemed to offer to Pilate once more a way of escape from his difficulty. It was the custom of the Roman governor on Passover morning to release to the people any single prisoner they might desire. It was a privilege highly prized by the populace of Jerusalem, for there were always in jail plenty of prisoners who, by rebellion against the detested foreign yoke, had made themselves the heroes of the multitude. At this stage of the trial of Jesus, the mob of the city, pouring from street and alley in the excited Oriental fashion, came streaming up the avenue to the front of the palace, shouting for this annual gift. (Mark 15:6-8)

The cry was for once welcome to Pilate, for he saw in it a loophole of escape from his disagreeable position. It turned out, however, to be a noose through which he was slipping his neck. He offered the life of Jesus to the mob. For a moment they hesitated. But they had a noted leader of revolt against the Roman domination; and besides, voices instantly began to whisper busily in their ears, putting every art of persuasion into exercise in order to induce them not to accept Jesus. The Sanhedrists, in spite of the zeal they had manifested the hour before for law and order, did not scruple thus to take the side of the champion of sedition; and they succeeded only too well in poisoning the minds of the populace, who began to shout for their own hero, Barabbas. (Mark 15:9-11)

"What, then, shall I do with Jesus?" asked Pilate, expecting them to answer, "Give us Him too." But he was

mistaken; the authorities had done their work success-
fully; the cry came from ten thousand throats, "Let Him
be crucified!" Pilate, completely baffled, angrily asked,
"Why, what evil hath He done?" But he had put the
decision into their power; they were now thoroughly fa-
naticized, and yelled forth, "Away with Him; crucify
Him, crucify Him!" (Matthew 27:15-23)

Pilate did not yet mean to sacrifice justice utterly. He
had still a move in reserve; but in the meantime He sent
away Jesus to be scourged—the usual preliminary to
crucifixion. The soldiers took Him to a room in their
barracks, and feasted their cruel instincts on His sufferings. When the scourging was over, they set Him down
on a seat, and, fetching an old cast-off cloak, flung it, in
derisive imitation of the royal purple, on His shoulders;
they thrust a reed into His hands for a scepter; they
stripped some thorn-twigs from a neighboring bush, and,
twining them into the rough semblance of a crown,
crushed down their rending spikes upon His brow. Then,
passing in front of Him, each of them in turn bent the
knee, while, at the same time, he spat in His face, and
plucking the reed from His hand, smote Him with it over
the head and face. (Matthew 27:26-31)

At last, having glutted their cruelty, they led Him back
to the tribunal, wearing the crown of thorns and the purple robe. The crowds raised shouts of mad laughter at
the soldiers' joke; and, with a sneer on his face, Pilate
thrust Him forward, so as to meet the gaze of all, and
cried, "Behold the man!" He meant that surely there
was no use of doing any more to Him; He was not worth
their while; could one so broken and wretched do any
harm? How little he understood his own words! That

"Ecce Homo" of his sounds over the world and draws the eyes of all generations to that marred visage. And lo, as we look, the shame is gone; it has lifted off Him and fallen on Pilate himself, on the soldiery, the priests, and the mob. His outflashing glory has scorched away every speck of disgrace, and tipped the crown of thorns with a hundred points of flaming brightness. But just as little did Pilate understand the temper of the people he ruled, when he supposed that the sight of the misery and helplessness of Jesus would satisfy their thirst for vengeance. The sight of Him now, scourged, raised their hate to madness, so that they cried louder than ever, "Crucify Him, crucify Him." (John 19:4-6)

Now at last, too, they gave vent to the real charge against Him, which had all along been burning at the bottom of their hearts, and which they could no longer suppress: "We have a law," they cried, "and by that law He ought to die, because He made Himself the Son of God." But these words struck a chord in Pilate's mind which they had not thought of. In the ancient traditions of his native land there were many legends of sons of the gods, who in the days of old had walked the earth in humble guise, so that they were indistinguishable from common men. In Jesus Pilate had discerned an inexplicable something which affected him with a vague terror. And now the words of the mob, "He made Himself the Son of God," came like a flash of lightning. Might not Jesus be the Son of the Hebrew Jehovah—so his heathen mind reasoned? He hastily took Him inside the palace again, and, looking at Him with new awe and curiosity, asked, "Whence art Thou? But Jesus answered him not one word. The proud governor was both surprised and irritated, and demanded, "Speakest Thou not to me? Knowest Thou not that I have power to crucify Thee, and have power to release Thee?" to which Jesus answered with the indescribable dignity of which the brutal shame of His torture had in no way robbed Him, "Thou couldst have no power at all against Me, except it were given thee from above." (John 19:7-11)

Pilate came forth from his private interview determined at once to release Him. The Jews saw it in His face; and it made them bring out their last weapon, which they had all along been keeping in reserve: they threatened to complain against him to the emperor. This was the meaning of the cry with which they interrupted his first words, "If thou let this man go, thou art not Cæsar's friend." There was nothing a Roman governor dreaded so much as a complaint against him sent by his subjects to the emperor. At this time it was specially perilous; for the imperial throne was occupied by a morbid and suspicious tyrant, who delighted in disgracing his own servants. Pilate knew too well that his administration could not bear inspection, for it had been cruel and corrupt in the extreme. This was the blast of temptation which finally swept Pilate off his feet, just when he had made up his mind to obey his conscience. He saw at once that he must surrender Jesus to their will. (John 19:12)

Calling for water, he washed his hands in the presence of the multitude, and cried, "I am innocent of the blood of this just Person." He washed his hands when he should have exerted them. Blood is not so easily washed off. But the mob, now completely triumphant, derided his scruples, rending the air with the cry, "His blood be upon us and on our children!"

Pilate felt the insult keenly, and, turning on them in his anger, determined that he, too, should have his triumph. Thrusting Jesus forward more prominently into view, he began to mock them by pretending to regard Him as really their king, and asking, "Shall I crucify your king?" It was now their turn to feel the sting of mockery; and they cried out, "We have no king but Cæsar." What a confession from Jewish lips! It was the surrender of the freedom and the history of the nation. Pilate took them at their word, and forthwith handed Jesus over to be crucified. (John 19:13-16)

THIRTEEN

Crucifixion,

Resurrection and Ascension

THE CRUCIFIXION

The religionists had succeeded in wresting their victim from Pilate's unwilling hands, "and they took Jesus and led Him away." At length they were able to gratify their hatred to the uttermost, and they hurried Him off to the place of execution with every demonstration of inhuman triumph. The actual executioners were the soldiers of the governor's guard; but in moral significance the deed belonged entirely to the Jewish authorities. They could not leave it in charge of the minions of the law to whom it belonged, but with undignified eagerness headed the procession themselves, in order to feast their vindictiveness on the sight of His sufferings. (John 19:16; Acts 2:36)

It must by this time have been about ten o'clock in the morning. The crowd at the palace had been gradually swelling. As the fatal procession, headed by the Sanhedrists, passed on through the streets, it attracted great multitudes. It happened to be a Passover holiday, so that there were thousands of idlers, prepared for any excitement. All those especially who had been inoculated with the fanaticism of the authorities poured forth to witness the execution. It was therefore through the midst of myriads of cruel and unsympathizing onlookers that Jesus went to His death. (Luke 23:27)

The spot where He suffered can not now be identified. It was outside the gates of the city, and was doubtless the common place of execution. The name Golgotha, "place of a skull," may signify a skull-like knoll, but more probably refers to the ghastly relics of the tragedies happening there that might be lying about. It was probably a wide, open space, in which a multitude of spectators might assemble; and it appears to have been on the side of a much frequented thoroughfare, for, besides the stationary spectators, there were others passing to and fro who joined in mocking the Sufferer. (Matthew 27:33)

Crucifixion was an unspeakably horrible death, the most cruel and shameful of all punishments. Nothing could be more unnatural and revolting than to suspend a living man in such a position. The idea of it seems to have been suggested by the practices of nailing up vermin in a kind of revengeful merriment on some exposed place. The victim usually lingered two or three days, with the burning pain of the nails in his hands and feet, the torture of overcharged veins, and, worst of all, his intolerable thirst, constantly increasing. It was impossible to help moving the body so as to get relief from each new attitude of pain; yet every movement brought new and excruciating agony. (Luke 23:33)

But we gladly turn away from the awful sight, to think how by His strength of soul, His resignation, and His love, Jesus triumphed over the shame, the cruelty, and horror of it; and how He converted the symbol of slavery and wickedness into a symbol for whatever is most pure and glorious in the world. The head hung free in crucifixion, so that He was able not only to see what was going on beneath Him, but also to speak. He uttered seven sentences at intervals, which have been preserved to us. They show that He retained unimpaired the serenity and majesty which had characterized Him throughout His trial, and exhibited in their fullest exercise all the qualities which had already made His character illustrious. He triumphed over His sufferings not by the cold severity of a Stoic, but by self-forgetting love. He was absorbed in a prayer for His murderers. He quenched the pain of the first hours of crucifixion by His interest in the penitent thief and His care to provide a new home for His mother. He never was more completely Himself—the absolutely unselfish Worker for others. (Luke 23:43,46; Matthew 27:46; John 19:27-30)

He did not linger more than five hours—a space of time so much briefer than usual, that the soldiers, who were about to break His legs, were surprised to find Him already dead. His worst sufferings were those of mind. He whose very life was love was encircled with a sea of hatred and of dark, bitter, hellish passion, that surged round Him. The members of the Sanhedrin took the lead in venting on Him every possible expression of contempt and malicious hate, and the populace faithfully followed their example. These were the men He had loved and still loved with an unquenchable passion; and they insulted, crushed, and trampled on His love. That seething mass of human beings, whose faces, distorted with passion, glared upon Him, was an epitome of the wickedness of the human race. His eyes had to look down on it, and its coarseness, its sadness, its dishonor of God, its exhibition of the shame of human nature were like a sheaf of spears gathered in His breast. (John 19:33; Luke 23:35-37)

There was a still more mysterious woe. Not only did the world's sin thus press itself on His loving and holy soul in those near Him; it came from afar,—from the past, the distant, and the future—and met on Him. He was bearing the sin of the world. So it pleased the Lord to put Him to grief, when He who knew no sin was made sin for us. (II Corinthians 5:12)

These were the sufferings which made the cross appalling. At the same time a strange darkness overspread the land, and Jerusalem trembled beneath a cloud whose murky shadows looked like a gathering doom. Golgotha was well-nigh deserted. At length, out of the depths of an anguish which human thought will never fathom, there issued the cry, "My God, my God, why hast Thou forsaken Me?" It was the moment when the soul of the Sufferer touched the very bottom of His misery. But with the strength of victory won in the final struggle, He cried, "It is finished!" and then, with perfect serenity, breathed out His life on a verse of a favorite psalm: "Father, into Thy hands I commend My spirit." (Luke 23:44-46; Matthew 27:46)

THE RESURRECTION AND ASCENSION

There never was an enterprise in the world which seemed more completely at an end than did that of Jesus on the last Old Testament Sabbath. The Jewish authorities were thoroughly satisfied of this. Death ends all controversies, and had settled the one between Him and them triumphantly in their favor. He had put Himself forward as their Messiah, but had scarcely any of the marks which they looked for in one with such claims. He had never received any important national recognition. His followers were few and uninfluential. His career had been short. He was in the grave. (Matthew 27:57-60)

The breakdown of the disciples had been complete. When He was arrested, "they all forsook Him and fled." Peter, indeed, followed Him to the high-priest's palace, but only to fall more ignominiously than the rest. John followed even to Golgotha, and may have hoped against hope that, at the last moment, He might descend from the cross to ascend the Messianic throne. But even the last moment went by with nothing done. What remained for them but to return to their homes and their fishing as disappointed men, who would be twitted during the rest of their lives with the folly of following a pretender, and asked where the thrones were which He had promised to seat them on? (Matthew 26:56)

Jesus had, indeed, foretold His sufferings, death, and resurrection. But they never understood these sayings; they forgot them or gave them an allegorical turn; and, when He was actually dead, these yielded them no comfort whatever. The women came to the sepulcher, not to see it empty, but to embalm His body for its long sleep. Mary ran to tell the disciples, not that He was risen, but that the body had been taken away and laid she knew not where. When the women told the other disciples how He had met them, "their words seemed to them as idle tales and they believed them not." Peter and John, as John himself informs us, "knew not the Scripture, that He should rise from the dead." Could anything be more pathetic than the words of the two travelers to Emmaus, "We trusted that it had been He which should have redeemed Israel?" When the disciples were met together, "they mourned and wept." There never were men more utterly disappointed and dispirited. (John 20:1-9; Luke 24:21)

But we can now be glad that they were so sad. For how is it to be accounted for, that in a few days afterwards these very men were full of confidence and joy, their faith in Jesus had revived, and the enterprise of Christianity was again in motion with a far vaster vitality than it had ever before possessed? They say the reason of this was that Jesus had risen, and they had seen Him. They tell us about their visit to the empty tomb, and how He appeared to Mary Magdalene, to the other women, to Peter, to the two on the way to Emmaus, to ten of them at once, to eleven of them at once, to James, to the five hundred, and so forth. Are these stories credible? They might not be, if they stood alone. But the alleged resurrection of Christ was accompanied by the indisputable resurrection of Christianity. And how is the latter to be accounted for except by the former? The remarkable thing is that, when they resumed their faith in Him, they were found to be no longer pursuing worldly ends, but intensely spiritual ones; they were no longer expecting thrones, but persecution and death; yet they addressed themselves to their new work with a breadth of intelligence, an ardor of devotion, and a faith in results which they had never shown before. As Christ rose from the dead in a transfigured body, so did Christianity. (Mark 16:1-14; Luke 24:24-48; I Corinthians 15:1-8)

What effected this change? They say it was the resurrection and the sight of the risen Christ. But their testimony is not the proof that He rose. The incontestable proof is the change itself,—the fact that suddenly they had become courageous, hopeful, believing, wise, and equipped with resources sufficient to found the church, convert the world, and establish Christianity in its purity among men. Between the last Old Testament Sabbath and the time, a few weeks afterwards, when this stupendous change had undeniably taken place, some event must have intervened which can be regarded as a sufficient cause for so great an effect. The resurrection alone answers the exigencies of the problem, and is therefore proved by a demonstration far more cogent than perhaps any testimony could be. For if Christ be not risen, our faith is vain; but if He be risen, then the whole of His miraculous life becomes credible, for this was the greatest of all the miracles; His divine mission is demonstrated, for it must have been God who raised Him up.

The risen Christ lingered on earth long enough fully to satisfy His adherents of the truth of His resurrection. They were not easily convinced. The apostles treated the reports of the holy women with scornful incredulity; Thomas doubted the testimony of the other apostles; and some of the five hundred to whom He appeared on a Galilean mountain doubted their own eyesight, and only believed when they heard His voice. The loving patience with which He treated these doubters showed that, though His bodily appearance was somewhat changed, He was still the same in heart as ever. (John 20:26-29)

Yet there were obvious indications that He belonged no more to this lower world. There was a new reserve about His risen humanity. He forbade Mary to touch Him, when she would have kissed His feet. He appeared in the

He forbade Mary to touch Him.

midst of His own with mysterious suddenness, and just as suddenly vanished out of sight. He was only now and then in their company, no longer according them the constant and familiar relationship of former days. At length, at the end of forty days, when the purpose for which He had lingered on earth was fully accomplished and the apostles were ready in the power of their new joy to bear to all nations the tidings of His life and work, His glorified humanity was received up into that world to which it rightfully belonged. (John 20:17; Luke 24:50-53)

CONCLUSION

No life ends even for this world when the body by which it has for a little been made visible disappears from the face of the earth. Indeed, the true magnitude of a human being can often only be measured by what this after-life shows him to have been. So it was with Christ. The modest narrative of the Gospels scarcely prepares us for the outburst of creative force which issued from His life when it appeared to have ended. His influence on the modern world is the evidence of how great He was; for there must have been in the cause as much as there is in the effect.

The most important evidence of what He was, is to be found neither in the general history of modern civilization nor in the public history of the church, but in the experiences of the succession of genuine believers. The experience of myriads of souls, redeemed by Him from themselves and from the world, proves that history was cut in twain by the appearance of a Regenerator, who was not a mere link in the chain of common men, but One whom the race could not from its own resources have produced—the perfect Type, the Man of men. The experience of myriads of consciences proves that in the midst of all ages there was wrought out an act of reconciliation by which sinful men may be made one with a holy God. The experience of myriads of minds, rendered blessed by the vision of a God who to the eye purified by the Word of Christ proves that the revelation of the Eternal to the world has been made by One who knew Him so well that He could not Himself have been less than Divine.